W9-DBT-122

the economics of
Public Issues

the economics of
Public Issues

Sixth Edition

Douglass C. North
UNIVERSITY OF WASHINGTON

Roger LeRoy Miller
UNIVERSITY OF MIAMI

1817

HARPER & ROW, PUBLISHERS, New York
Cambridge, Philadelphia, San Francisco,
London, Mexico City, São Paulo, Sydney

RECEIVED
JUN 1 2 1984
MSU - LIBRARY

HB
34
.N6
1983

Sponsoring Editor: David Forgione
Project Coordinator: Irene Gunther
Production Manager: Kewal K. Sharma
Compositor: Allen Wayne
Printer and Binder: The Murray Printing Company

THE ECONOMICS OF PUBLIC ISSUES, Sixth Edition

Copyright © 1983 by Harper & Row, Publishers, Inc.

All rights reserved. Printed in the United States of America. No part of this
book may be used or reproduced in any manner whatsoever without written
permission, except in the case of brief quotations embodied in critical articles
and reviews. For information address Harper & Row, Publishers, Inc.,
10 East 53d Street, New York, NY 10022.

Library of Congress Cataloging in Publication Data

North, Douglass Cecil.
    The economics of public issues.

    Includes index.
        1. Economics—Addresses, essays, lectures.   2. Industry
and state—Addresses, essays, lectures.   3. Economic
policy—Addresses, essays, lectures.   I. Miller, Roger
LeRoy, 1942–   . II. Title.
HB34.N6   1983   330.973′092   82-23356
ISBN 0-06-044848-2

Contents

587706

Preface

Economists cannot tell people what they ought to do. They can only expose the costs and benefits of various alternatives so that citizens in a democratic society can make better choices. In this book, we present the interested reader with some ideas of what the costs and benefits are for various proposed social actions. Economic issues surround us in our daily lives, in our work and in our play. Often, we may not even be aware of the extent to which economics affects public issues. Nonetheless, it plays a large role in most public issues, whether we are talking about water, illegal drugs, crime prevention, higher education, or professional sports.

For students first taking an introductory economics course, this book is offered as a supplement to the main text. Reading it in conjunction with a book that explains economic theory in detail can demonstrate both the relevance of that theory and the way in which it can be used to analyze the world around us. No a priori knowledge of economics is necessary for understanding any of the chapters in this book. Necessarily, then, the reader must be warned that in no case is our treatment of a topic exhaustive. We have merely attempted to expose the bare economic bones of some aspects of the issues treated. Further class discussion will undoubtedly reveal the more complex nature of those issues.

For professors using this book, we have prepared a short *Instructor's Manual* which we think is useful. It contains a lecture outline of each chapter, graphical explanations, questions for additional thought and discussion, and selected references. It is available from the publisher on request.

When we began to plan the sixth edition, we asked Harper & Row to do a survey of users of *The Economics of Public Issues*. The results of that survey were indeed surprising. A large number of users requested that we reinstate some of the issues that had appeared in the fourth and fifth editions. Others suggested the addition of new topics. Still others recommended that we do virtually nothing except update the fifth edition. Consequently, we reached a compromise. This edition includes several new economic issues, among them the stock market, water, auto congestion, and cents-off coupons. Also, some issues from previous editions have been reintroduced, such as income distribution and government programs, as well as ecology and income distribution. Finally, the remaining issues have been updated and revised wherever necessary.

In this edition, we have added a set of pedagogical devices to help the student reader better understand the economic analysis that applies to each part and chapter. These devices are as follows:

1. An introductory explanation precedes each of the five parts. Where applicable, economic terms are set in boldface in these sections.
2. Economic terms are set in boldface the first time they appear in the text. All boldface terms are defined in a glossary at the end of the text.

3. Each chapter contains a concluding summary paragraph clearly stating the economic principles covered in the chapter.
4. Each chapter ends with discussion questions suitable for classroom use.

Through the years, many instructors have given us ideas, suggestions, and criticisms. For this edition, we were able to obtain the helpful written comments of the following reviewers: John F. Stehle, Villanova University; Eleanor D. Craig, University of Delaware; Bassam Harik, Western Michigan University; Marcia Frost Watkins, Pepperdine University; David Easley, Cornell University; Richard V. Burkhauser, Vanderbilt University; John H. Haehl, California State University at Fullerton; Michael K. Mischaikow, Western Washington University; Gaston V. Rimlinger, Rice University.

To these reviewers, we wish to express our sincere appreciation for their numerous helpful comments. We also wish to thank the many other instructors who have written us. As always, we take responsibility for any remaining errors. We continue to welcome all comments and suggestions for change.

Douglass C. North
Roger LeRoy Miller

part one
Supply and Demand

INTRODUCTION

Supply and demand analysis forms the basis of virtually all economic analysis. In this part, we look at a number of issues, some of which do not appear to lend themselves to economic analysis. Nonetheless, each and every issue does, in fact, have an economic aspect. As you read about energy, illicit drugs, agricultural products, and water, for example, you will find that supply and demand analysis applies throughout.

While reading about these issues, keep in mind the following:

1. The **law of demand** and the **law of supply** are given, holding other things constant.
2. A change in price affects quantities demanded and supplied. A change in any other nonprice variable shifts the entire demand or supply curve; in other words, there is a clear distinction between quantity demanded and supplied and demand and supply.
3. The laws of supply and demand relate price per **constant quality unit** to quantities supplied and demanded.

It is not necessary for everyone to react to price changes for the laws of demand and supply to be valid; the only requirement is that *some* marginal buyers or marginal producers react to price changes. In economics, all movement is on the margin.

1

the economics of
Energy

The question concerning the duration of our present cheap supplies of _____ cannot but excite deep interest and anxiety. . . . The constant tendency of discovery is to render _____ a more and more efficient agent, while there is no probability that when our _____ is used up any more powerful substitute will be forthcoming. . . . We cannot make up for a future want of _____ by importation from other countries. . . . Considering how greatly our (industrial capacity) depends upon _____ and how vast is our consumption of it compared with that of other nations, it cannot be supposed that we shall do without _____ more than a fraction of what we do with it. . . . It is then simply inferred that we cannot long continue our present rate of progress.

What is the magic word that should be inserted in the blanks in the above quotation? Most people would guess oil, for that is a continued subject of concern in the world today, particularly since the energy crisis of 1973–1974, which was touched off by a general embargo imposed by Middle Eastern countries on the shipment of oil to the United States, Europe, and the Far East.

When do you think that quotation was written: probably within the last decade, certainly since 1973, or perhaps 10 or 15 years ago by someone who predicted the future very well? You would be wrong on all counts. If you insert the word "coal" instead of "oil" wherever there is a blank, you will have an exact quotation from a book called *The Coal Question*, written by an English economist, William Stanley Jevons. That book was not published in 1975 or even in 1900; it was published in 1865. In 1865, this famous economist was saying exactly the same things about coal that people are saying today about oil. He was an expert and he was proven wrong: today, recoverable reserves of coal are estimated to be equivalent to 12 *trillion* barrels of oil. To understand why Jevons' prediction did not come true is to understand the roots of our current energy problems. What we need to look at is both the supply of energy and the demand for energy. First let's look at the supply.

Energy comes in many forms. Today we are familiar with natural gas, oil, coal, nuclear power, and, to a lesser extent, solar energy. But we have had other forms of energy in the past. After all, petroleum wasn't discovered until 1859. At one time, even whale oil was an important source of energy. This is a good place to start our discussion of the root causes of energy crises.

Before electricity was used to light our houses and our streets, the major source of artificial lighting, not only in Europe but also in the United States, was whale oil. At that time, there were no good substitutes for this oil as a source of light. Hence, the entire world supply of light, except for the sun and moon, depended almost entirely on the whaling industry. We didn't have many sophisticated models then to tell us what the whale oil **deficit** was going to be, although people knew it had to come about sooner or later. After all, the supply of whales couldn't forever keep pace with the increases in demand.

During the Civil War, the demand for whale oil increased tremendously. Moreover, the supply fell abruptly, for there were war-caused disruptions in the production process.[1] Whaling vessels were conscripted as freight ships. Additionally, southern privateers captured or destroyed many of the whaling ships that had not been conscripted. The result—a 50 percent drop in the number of American whaling ships, and a 60 percent drop in total tonnage. The crisis of artificial lighting fuel was clearly upon the nation.

Strangely enough, however, no crisis was ever talked about in the pubs or homes. What people talked about was the horrible rise in the price of whale oil. It cost so much more to read at night that some people decided it wasn't worth it. Sperm whale oil rose from 43 cents a gallon in 1823 to a whopping $2.55 a gallon in 1866. The high price of whale oil caused several things to happen. People started conserving whale oil because it was too expensive to waste. Another thing happened which is rarely remembered. As prices rose, the incentive for entrepreneurs to develop **substitutes** also rose. In Europe, gas that was distilled from coal suddenly became an economically feasible substitute, thus causing the quantity of whale oil demanded to drop off sharply. And since petroleum had been discovered in Pennsylvania, it was just a matter of time until the high price of whale oil would induce profit-seeking businesspersons to develop some sort of efficient refining process for crude oil.

So what happened was bound to happen. In 1867, kerosene became a cheap substitute for whale oil. By 1896, sperm whale oil was the cheapest it had been for many decades, a mere 40 cents a gallon. But very few people used it for lighting, even at that price. Whale oil lamps disappeared. The petroleum age was upon us.

Without going into detail, the same discussion can be applied to Britain's shift from wood to coal. Up to the 1400s, most people in Britain scoffed at the idea that there could be a **shortage** of trees. Nonetheless, from about 1550 to 1625, deforestation of the British Isles was brought about by the expansion of agricultural industry and trade. This, coupled with a doubling of the population, indeed made wood more and more scarce. The result,

---

[1] The demand curve shifted out; the supply curve shifted in.

of course, was that the price of wood rose much more rapidly than almost all other prices. By 1640, Londoners depended on coal to heat their homes despite the grime it created. Craftspersons who used to turn their noses up at coal fires because the smoke tarnished their wares were now burning coal almost exclusively. By 1700, the British Isles had almost completely converted to coal.

The discussion of whale oil and petroleum, and of wood and coal, can be carried over to the energy problems that have faced the United States—and indeed the rest of the world—in the 1970s and 1980s. A rise in petroleum prices should elicit a supply response. At some higher price of petroleum, alternatives such as solar energy, shale oil, and the like, will become competitive. Indeed, at a high enough price of petroleum, it might be economically sensible to use wind and wave power. Price also has an effect on the demand side. At higher prices of petroleum products, individuals will usually react by using less of them. After all, that is the first fundamental **law of demand**—there is an inverse relationship between quantity demanded and the price of the good in question, other things held constant. In other words, when the price of petroleum relative to all other prices—its **relative price**—goes up, the quantity demanded will fall.

Note here that we use the term *relative price.* Another way to think of the appropriate price is to call it the **real price,** for we do have to take account of inflation. When people talk about the "high" price of gasoline today, they often forget that all prices are high today relative to what they were in years past, for we have been experiencing rapid rates of **inflation** for the last 10 years. If the price per gallon of regular gas was 31 cents in 1960 and it rose to 63 cents in 1977, that is an increase of 103.2 percent. But during that same period, the average of all prices rose by 103.1 percent. Thus, the real, or relative, price of gas to the consumer in 1977 was about what is was in 1960. It's not surprising, then, that the quantity of gasoline demanded hasn't fallen very much due to the supposed high prices.

We have, however, seen radical shifts in both supply and demand in the energy field in the last few years. The now famous

Organization of Petroleum Exporting Countries—a group of oil producers mainly in the Persian Gulf—was successful in imposing an embargo on the shipment of OPEC oil to large sectors of the world. This occurred after the outbreak of war in the Middle East in 1973. Since then, OPEC, acting to benefit its member countries, has basically cut back on production and effectively raised prices. (Remember, the only way to raise prices is to cut back on production and sales.) The OPEC price of oil from Saudi Arabia was $2.12 a barrel on January 1, 1973. By 1982, the price had risen to $32.42.

When the supply of a product is reduced without a concomitant reduction in demand, the predicted result is a rise in price. In other words, when the **supply curve** shifts in, unaccompanied by an equal shift inward of the **demand curve,** the price rises. But, immediately after the reduction in supply in 1973, the price of petroleum products in the United States was not allowed to rise because of the price controls then in effect. We experienced actual shortages, queuing, and numerous "out of gas" signs because of those controls. When they were lifted in the spring of 1974, lines at gas stations quickly disappeared. But price controls on U.S. crude oil, together with a maze of regulations and controls on refineries, have kept the U.S. price of oil below the world price. This is one reason why U.S. consumption has not fallen. The controls on so-called "old oil" in the United States have discouraged its production. Simultaneously, the artificially low prices have caused increased consumption which, coupled with reduced U.S. production, has increased the demand for imported oil.

What does the future hold? The answer can be found by looking at the supply response to the new higher price of world oil. The long-run **price elasticity of supply** seems to be very great indeed. Let's take just a few examples.

Since the end of 1973, worldwide crude oil production has amounted to about 90 billion barrels. New proven reserve *additions* have exceeded 110 billion barrels; thus, a decade after the big scarcity threat of 1973–1974, new proven reserves are being added faster than production. In other words, the world's proven reserve inventory continues to increase. Also consider the fact that, up until World War II, U.S. oil production accounted for 70 percent of the world production of oil, even though it had at that time only about 12 percent of the recoverable conventional crude oil proven reserves in the world. Since World War II, the United States has still accounted for over one-third of cumulative production. That means that the rest of the world hasn't done much yet with the oil that it has in the ground. To date, less than 10 percent of the non-U.S. conventional oil-resource proven reserves has been produced. The higher price of oil has already elicited big finds in the North Sea, off the coast of Greece, and off the coast of Mexico. If history is any indication of the future, we will continue to see increased worldwide output because of the now higher prices of oil.

In sum, the planet's accessible reserves of hydrocarbon energy exceed the equivalent of some 20 trillion barrels of oil. This is the equivalent of five centuries of consumption at current rates. It is hard to imagine that we are seriously thinking about running out of energy in the near future.

We also have to look at what has happened to the real price of energy during the last decade. When we talk about real price, we mean that we are correcting for inflation. For example, if the price of gasoline was 30 cents in 1950 and 60 cents in 1970, its **nominal**, or **absolute**, price has gone up 100 percent. If all other prices also went up 100 percent, its real, or relative, price will have remained the same. As a matter of fact, the real price of energy fell by almost 20 percent from 1950 to 1970. This means that, in general, the average of all prices in the United States went up about 30 percent more than the price of energy. When we look at what has happened to the real price of OPEC oil since the embargo of 1973–1974, we find that it has risen very little. How could that be, you say? The price of gas at the gas pump seems to be going up all the time. That is correct, but that is exactly what you expect to see during an inflationary period. Inflation is defined as a rise in the weighted average of all prices. You expect the price of gasoline to go up, too.

In spite of the many predictions of continuing shortages of petroleum products, the world was awash with oil by 1982. Indeed, during some months of 1981 and 1982, the nominal price of gasoline at the pump actually fell. Of course, those who are convinced that oil is a special product, not subject to standard economic analysis, maintain that the 1982 **surplus** of crude oil will soon disappear and shortages will again occur.

SUMMARY

The energy picture is certainly more complex than we have been able to describe in the last few pages, but the basic analysis will always be the same. When the price of one energy source goes up, consumers will be induced to cut back and suppliers will be induced to produce more. If the price is expected to stay up, alternative energy sources will be developed more rapidly. The laws of supply and demand apply to energy just as they apply to food, clothing, and just about any other good or service you might wish to study.

DISCUSSION QUESTIONS

1. How is it possible to have had "gas shortages" in the 1970s and then reductions in the nominal price of gasoline at the pump in the 1980s?
2. Why did we have long lines at gas stations in 1973–1974?
3. Is it possible to physically run out of all energy sources? Why or why not?

2

the economics of
Euphoria

Marijuana is normally illegal; so are hashish, mescaline, dimethyltriptamine, psilocybin, and tetrahydrocannabinol. The illegality of these drugs does not, of course, prevent their use by young and old alike. It does, however, add certain peculiar characteristics to their production, distribution, and usage.

Before we look at drugs, we can learn a few things by examining a historical experience that proved unforgettable to most who lived through it—Prohibition.

On January 16, 1920, the Eighteenth Amendment to the United States Constitution became effective. It prohibited the "manufacture, sale, or transportation of intoxicating liquors within, or the import into, or export from the United States for beverage purposes." The Volstead Act, passed in 1919 to reinforce the Eighteenth Amendment, forbade the purchase, possession, and use of intoxicating liquors.[1]

A once-legal commodity became illegal overnight. The results were impressive, but they certainly could have been predicted by any economist. Since the legal supply of liquor and wine fell to practically zero and much of the public continued to demand the commodity, substitutes were quickly provided. Supplies of illegal liquor and wine flowed into the market. Increasing quantities of whiskey clandestinely found their way across the border from Canada, where its production was legal.

Of course, fewer entrepreneurs were now willing to provide the U.S. public with liquor. Why? Mainly because the cost of doing business suddenly increased. Potential speakeasy operators had to take into account a high risk of being jailed and/or fined. They also faced increased costs in operating a bar, for the usual business matters had to be carried on in a surreptitious (i.e., more costly) way. Moreover, speakeasy operators had to face the inevitable: an encounter with organized crime. They could look forward to paying off organized crime in addition to the local cops. Payments to the former reduced the possibility of cement shoes and the East River. Payments to the latter reduced the probability of landing in jail.

As a general summation, it could be said that Prohibition probably decreased the amount of alcoholic beverages that entrepreneurs were willing to provide *at the same prices as before.* If a bottle of one's favorite Scotch was available for $3 in 1919, either it would have cost more in 1920, or it would have been filled with a lower-quality product.

Whiskey lovers faced another problem during Prohibition. They could no longer search for the newspaper ads and billboards

[1] Wine intended for religious purposes was excepted. A report of the Federal Council of the Churches of Christ in America showed that nearly 3 million gallons of sacramental wine were withdrawn in 1924 from government warehouses. This leads to interesting speculation about whether Prohibition somehow made Americans suddenly more religious.

to find the best buys in bourbon. Information had gone underground, and even knowledge about quality and price had suddenly become a much dearer commodity. In general, consumers have several means of obtaining information. They can find out about products from friends, from advertisements, and from personal experience. When goods are legal, they can be trademarked for identification. The trademark cannot be copied, and the courts protect it. Given such easily identified brands, consumers can be made aware of the quality and price of each via the recommendations of friends and ads. If their experience with a product does not jibe with their anticipations, they can assure themselves of no further encounter with the "bad" product by never buying that brand again.

When a general class of products becomes illegal, there are fewer ways of obtaining information on product quality. Brand names are no longer protected by the law; so falsification of well-known ones ensues. It becomes difficult to determine which trademarks are the "best." We therefore can understand why some unfortunate imbibers were blinded or killed by the effects of bad whiskey. The risk of something far more serious than a hangover became very real.

For some, the new whiskey-drinking costs were outweighed by the illicit joys of the speakeasy atmosphere. But other drinkers with more sensitive ethics were repelled by liquor's illegality and were deterred from consuming as much as they had before Prohibition, even if the liquor were obtainable at the same price as before.

While it is difficult to assess the net effect of these considerations, one fact is clear. Prohibition differed in its impact on the rich and the poor.

High-income drinkers were not particularly put out at having to pay more for the kind of whiskey they wanted. They ran little risk of being blinded, because neither the high price tag nor the cost of obtaining information about quality and supply could separate them from their favorite beverage. Presumably they would have been quite willing, before Prohibition, to pay more than the going price.

On the contrary, some lower-income imbibers had probably been paying just about their top limit for whiskey of acceptable quality before Prohibition. The sudden rise in price left them two alternatives: do without or settle for less, in the form of bootleg booze and bathtub gin. The distribution of injury, sickness, and death due to drinking contaminated whiskey directly mirrored the distribution of income.

There is an obvious analogy between what happened during Prohibition (the "noble experiment") and what is now happening with respect to most euphorics and hallucinogens. Like bootleg liquor, these drugs share the stricture of illegality which leads to both relatively high costs and high risk in their manufacture, distribution, sale, and consumption.[2] Yet there is a difference between the two periods in the matter of who obtains the more-wanted product. The wealthy user still is able to buy quality; he or she may even pay intermediaries to do the necessary shopping around. But while the middle-income user ends up getting inferior drugs, it seems likely that the "heads," or high-consumption users, who are almost always poor, often get hold of the better-quality euphorics, and often at prices below those paid by others. The reason for this situation involves a mixture of economics and sociology. First, these users are poor because they are working at low-paying jobs—if they are working at all. Therefore, when they spend time away from their jobs, not much is lost. Thus, we say that the opportunity cost of their not working is low compared to the opportunity cost of those with higher-paying jobs who must sacrifice more earnings when they choose not to work. The "poor" user merely responds to the low opportunity cost when he or she spends more time seeking out the best buys in the urgently wanted drugs. This was true during Prohibition, also, but it didn't have as much import because there did not exist such a large sociological class of "heads" devoted to the whiskey "cult."

On the other hand, the problems that face a middle-income drug user are manifold. If this user spends time seeking out infor-

[2] Although a number of states have in many ways "decriminalized" the use and possession of small quantities of marijuana.

mation about which euphorics to buy and where to find them, he or she is confronted with higher opportunity costs from time spent away from work. Potential jailing is a greater deterrent in terms of both opportunity costs and psychic and emotional costs. And since this individual is probably unable or unwilling to pay some intermediary to do the necessary searching (as the rich user would do), he or she will end up with drugs whose quality would be scorned by many low-income "heads."

Since the use of certain drugs is legal in other countries, why don't rich users fly overseas to obtain and use their drugs? Take the case of Nepal, where high-quality marijuana can be purchased for about 2 cents an ounce, while the price in the United States may run as high as $40 for the same quality and quantity. The relative price of the Nepalese euphoric is thus 1/2000 that of the U.S. euphoric. Or is it? When we consider the *total* cost, we see that we must include round-trip air fare to Nepal, plus the opportunity cost of the flight time (minus any monetary value placed on seeing that exotic country). The relative price of one ounce of legal Nepalese marijuana now becomes more like $\frac{\$.02 + \$800}{\$40} = 20$ times the U.S. price for illegal marijuana.[3]

Up to now we've been dealing mainly with the demand side of the illegal drug picture. We have looked at the determinants of how much people buy and how much they are willing to pay for a certain quality of euphorics. Now let's look briefly at the supply side. We wish to find out what determines how much people are willing to furnish of a certain quality of euphoric at different prices. This is known as the **law of supply.** The parallels to be made with the supply of whiskey during Prohibition are numerous. The illegality of the manufacture and distribution of most drugs poses a large risk to suppliers. The risk is higher the greater (1) the probability of detection, (2) the probability of conviction,

---

[3] The added cost to the user of detection, conviction, and jail are, of course, not included in the $40 price for the U.S. euphoric. However, the probability of detection and the costs of conviction are sufficiently low in the United States so as not to induce anyone to pay 20 times more for the pleasure of smoking marijuana in Nepal without fear of arrest.

and (3) the potential jail sentence and/or fine. Costs of doing business include measures to assure secrecy and avoid detection, payoffs to organized crime (for certain drugs not easily manufactured, like heroin), and potential payoffs to the police.

What would happen if marijuana were legalized? Should we expect a state of euphoria?

On the supply side, entrepreneurs would be able to supply larger quantities at the same price as before because the costs of doing business would fall. There would be no risks involved, no need for payoffs to organized crime, and no high cost of maintaining secrecy in production and distribution. The price would eventually fall to a level just covering the lower costs of legal production and legal distribution. In fact, we could even get more *cannabis* supplied if we were to repeat what happened in the colonial period. Then the English parliament established a bounty to encourage American planters to produce hemp, or *cannabis sativa*, the plant from which marijuana is produced. At that time *cannabis sativa* was a valuable article of American commerce. The seeds were used for oil, and the stalks of the plant could be fashioned into webbing, twine, bagging, and rope. The hemp fibers added durability to any material with which it was interwoven. The crop was important enough for King James I of England to declare it illegal for any settler who had hemp seeds not to plant them!

When there is unrestrained **competition** among the sellers of a legal product, it is difficult for relatively inferior products to exist side by side with better ones unless the price of the former is lower. Otherwise sellers of the superior product will inform the buying public of the anomaly. Since the product is legal, the free flow of information will assure that some buyers will refuse to purchase inferior products unless their price is correspondingly lower.

By opening the door to advertising, legalization would also reduce the costs of disseminating and obtaining information about supplies. Competition among sellers and increased information available to buyers would combine to raise the quality of the product.

On the demand side, legalization would, of course, eliminate the threats of detection, conviction, and jail, with their attendant costs. Because of higher overall quality, the risk of bad side effects from improperly prepared drugs would be lessened. Both of these cost reductions would lead consumers to demand a larger quantity even at the prices that had prevailed before legalization.

It is difficult to predict whether the price of marijuana would rise or fall immediately after legalization. Since consumers presumably would demand more, suppliers would produce more. If the increase in demand were to exceed that in supply, a shortage would result and consumers would find themselves paying high prices to obtain as much of the now-legal product as they wanted. In the long run, however, it could safely be predicted that prices would, as usual, fall to a level just covering the costs of production, distribution, and normal profit—which would certainly be lower than the price paid today. (In fact, given worldwide availability, we can safely assume that the supply of drugs in the United States is highly elastic at the approximate cost of production.)

If euphoric drugs in general were to be legalized and this chain of events occurred, one more link in the sequence would be a fall in the price of euphorics relative to that of alcoholic beverages. Would this lead to a trend away from drinking—and toward the smoking of marijuana, for example? The answer hinges on an "if." If marijuana is a *substitute* for alcohol, this might well happen. But if the two are **complementary** instead of substitutable, then increased use of marijuana would lead to increased use of alcohol.

In any event, the above analysis does not constitute an argument for or against legalization of euphorics. There are costs to society involved in each course. There are also benefits. Describing the costs of making something illegal does not necessarily argue for a change in the law. After all, there are costs involved in passing a law that forbids wife abandonment, but society obviously has decided that the benefits of making abandonment illegal far outweigh those costs.

SUMMARY

When a good or activity becomes illegal, there is typically a supply response and a demand response. Since illegality causes the cost of production to rise, the supply (curve) of an illegal good or activity will decrease. (The supply curve will shift inward to the left.) That means that a smaller quantity of the illegal good will be supplied at each and every price. On the demand side, we can predict that there will be some decrease in demand. (The demand curve will also shift inward to the left.) Historically in such cases, the supply decrease has been greater than the demand decrease, so that the **market-clearing price** of the illegal good is greater than the market-clearing price of the legal good.

DISCUSSION QUESTIONS

1. Does supply and demand analysis apply equally well to so-called hard, or addictive, drugs, such as heroin?
2. What effect does the inability to advertise have on the variability of price per constant quality unit of an illegal good?

3

the economics of
Prostitution

In 1945, a French politician—one Mme. Marthe Richards—demanded closure of all Paris brothels. She claimed that the 178 licensed houses, 600 prostitute-serving hotels, 10,000 pimps, and 6000 ladies of the night were "undermining Parisian morals and health." Moreover, she estimated that the closing of brothels would make available 6000 rooms for students and those bombed out of their homes during the war.

The Municipal Council of Paris, impressed by her statistics, gave the brothels three months to shut down. The effects have been far-reaching, to say the least, and apparently have not proved too satisfactory, because recently a vigorous campaign has been shaping up in France to restore the legality of the world's oldest profession. Although the product differs considerably, the economic analysis of prostitution is similar to that of euphoria, with, of course, a few special twists.

The service that prostitutes offer for sale has, like all others, two dimensions: quantity and quality. In some sense, these two are interrelated; quantity can be increased by lowering quality. The quality of the service is, among other things, a function of (1) experience (*human capital investment*);[1] (2) the innate characteristics of the provider of the service, such as looks and intelligence; and (3) current operating expenditures, such as how much money is spent on appearance, surroundings, and health.

To be sure, *substitution* is possible among these three aspects of quality. Perhaps the same quality can be achieved either by being born beautiful or by spending effort and money on makeup and clothes. Some ladies of the night are able to compensate for poor looks by dressing well. In economic terms, they are able to substitute clothes for natural endowments.

For many who utilize the services of a prostitute, the health aspect of quality is of utmost importance. The decision to make prostitution illegal in France had notable consequences on the probability of some clients contracting venereal disease. Let's see why.

When prostitution was legal, numerous business establishments existed whose purpose in life was offering prostitutes' services. Since all was on the up-and-up, they could advertise without risk. Because clients could easily compare prices and qualities, information was relatively cheap. If it became common knowledge that the employees of one house spread venereal disease to their customers, that firm would either have to lower its prices drastically or suffer a drop in clientele.

Even though cheap information made it inadvisable for any firm to allow unhealthy employees to work (because clients would go elsewhere), the French government made doubly sure that venereal disease was kept at a minimum by requiring weekly medical inspections. Since most prostitutes worked in establishments, it was relatively easy to check all of them, and social disease was rare among prostitutes before 1947. The reader can easily

---

[1] You are making an investment in your own human capital by attending college and by reading this book.

draw the analogy between legalized prostitution and legalized narcotic usage.

When prostitution was legal, suppliers of the service charged their opportunity cost, with no "risk" factor added, since no threat of imprisonment or fines existed. Those demanding the service had no need to invest large amounts of their resources (time and effort) obtaining information that would help them avoid the risk of a poor-quality product, as represented by the threat of venereal disease.

What has happened in France since 1947? Obviously there are no more legal houses of prostitution. The girls, for the most part, have taken to the streets. The cost of doing business has increased. Streetwalkers must avoid detection and arrest either by cleverness or by paying off police. Some girls must stay outside more than before, adding a cost of discomfort. Also, they no longer benefit from the **economies of scale** that previously kept down the cost of such "accessories" to their trade as an attractive atmosphere. At the same wages as before, then, fewer prostitutes were willing to stay in the profession after 1947. (Thus, the **supply schedule** shifted inward to the left.)

On the demand side, clients could no longer be so confident about the quality of the product, because competition among legal houses was removed. Previously, any house that got a bad reputation suffered. But now individual prostitutes can more easily lower quality (i.e., have V.D.) and still obtain clients, for information has become much more difficult to obtain. And, of course, there are no longer government medical inspections. (Such a situation would be roughly equivalent to a system of FDA inspection and labeling of different grades of marijuana in our own country.)

Predictably, as information about quality has become more expensive, the wealthy citizen has been the one able to pay the cost of seeking out the healthy prostitutes, while the poor have contracted venereal disease. But the cost of illegal prostitution affects others in the society. If a middle-class marijuana user dies from some arsenic in an illegal cigarette, the rest of society bears little of the cost. But if a dock worker contracts V.D., he is not alone in bearing the cost, because he can spread the disease to others. This explains in part why there is currently so much fervor in France about legalizing prostitution again: the rates of V.D. have soared among those associated with the prostitution industry, suppliers and demanders alike.

SUMMARY

The prohibiting of prostitution in France caused a decrease in the number (or growth rate) and in the average quality of prostitutes, probably a decrease in the number of demanders (even at the same prices as before), and probably a rise in the average price to the customer. As an added effect, V.D. became more common among common folk.

DISCUSSION QUESTIONS

1. What similarities are there between the economic analysis of prostitution and the economic analysis of illegal euphoric drugs?
2. Predict the results of legalization of prostitution throughout the United States. What if prostitution were legalized only in major cities?

4

the economics of
Safer Products

Coke bottles that explode in people's faces. Electric can openers that electrocute. Rotary mowers that amputate the hand of the operator. Nightgowns that burn the wearer to death. Cars that crash without warning because they are put together wrong. The number of product-related accidents is staggering. The cost of these bizarre mishaps is even more so, for the income lost by those injured, maimed, and dead as a result of fateful products mounts fast. Recently there has been a movement to protect consumers against unsafe products. In fact, the Consumer Product Safety Commission has been functioning for some time now. Its job is to oversee the level of product safety in the United States — to guarantee, presumably, that people will not bear any "undue" risk when they drive their cars, mow their lawns, or drink a beer. To analyze the effectiveness of legislation to improve product safety, it might help to look at the level of safety that would be dictated in an unrestricted market situation.

Let's take the example of an electric toothbrush manufacturing firm. Suppose it is the first one to enter the market. How does it decide how safe to make its toothbrushes? It would be nice to think it would make them absolutely safe, but absolute safety is not possible. If it were, however, it wouldn't come free of charge. Making a product safer usually involves a higher cost of production, and that usually results in a higher price, which in turn lowers the quantity demanded. Our electric toothbrush manufacturing firm probably knows this. At first, it has no information on what level of safety the public demands, so it might arbitrarily pick one. Let's say that one buyer in 50,000 gets electrocuted. This, of course, raises the true cost of the toothbrush to all users because of the probability of their suffering egregious harm some morning when they can't even see clearly into the bathroom mirror.

Now suppose another manufacturing firm comes along and believes that that level of safety is insufficient. This firm wants to make an electric toothbrush that will electrocute only one in every 150,000 users. Its cost of production may be a little higher, but it advertises that its product is safer. If it is correct in assuming that the market demand for safety is greater than that actually provided by the first toothbrush manufacturing firm, it will end up getting a larger share of the business. The first firm will have to follow suit if it wishes to compete; otherwise it will eventually go out of business.

In fact what probably would happen is that some consumers would prefer a cheaper, even if somewhat less safe, product and others would prefer a more expensive one with greater safety. As a result, as the electric toothbrush market expanded, there would be different submarkets with different price/quality combinations reflecting consumers' subjective tradeoff between price and safety.

This, then, is the mechanism by which the level of product safety desired by the public is discovered by manufacturers. It is a trial-and-error system that is not completely accurate at any point in time because information is never perfect. The key aspects of this argument are that the level of product safety will be demand-determined—that is, determined by the buyers of the product—in this particular situation, and that competition among producers will indeed result in the so-called optimal level of product safety.

But this optimal level of safety assumes that all consumers are informed about the risks that they take and can make a rational decision about the price/safety combination that they desire. We know, however, that information is not free. As such products become more complex and more numerous, the costs become significant and the consumer becomes more bewildered. This is the rationale for government safety regulations. Let's see how they work in the case of the automobile.

The automobile is the product that has had the most legislation with respect to its safety or lack of same. Safety legislation was prompted by the discoveries Ralph Nader exposed to the world in 1965 in his book *Unsafe at Any Speed*. He later testified at congressional hearings. Congress and the President were impressed enough to pass legislation setting up the National Highway Safety Bureau, later renamed the National Highway Traffic Safety Administration. Most people are aware of the numerous regulations that automobile manufacturers must now follow: dual brakes, double-laminated glass, no interior protrusions, over-the-shoulder seat belts, possibly required airbag passive restraint systems, and so on. We have no doubt that new automobiles are safer than they would be in the absence of such legislation, and that their occupants will sustain fewer injuries than they would have otherwise. However, we are talking only about the supply side of safety for automobiles. The supply of new automobiles is indeed safer. But the price of new automobiles is higher too. Let's see why by looking at the costs of making a Mustang or a Malibu.

There are certain costs that the manufacturing firm must incur no matter how many or how few new-model cars it sells. These costs include, initially, design and marketing research to determine what will sell best. Once the decision is made to produce a certain model, the costs of tooling up—that is, making new body dies, jigs, features, and new engine tools and molds—must be considered. Then follow all the costs of setting up the production line for the new car. And if the new model is to be accepted by the public, it has to be introduced via promotion (i.e., TV ads, billboards, and radio commercials), which involves costs.

All of the above are called **fixed costs** or **sunk costs**. Once they have been incurred by the auto manufacturer, they are gone forever, whether the car is bought by 100 people or by 100,000.

In addition to these costs, there are others that vary according to the number of cars produced, the most obvious being for labor and material inputs. The more cars made, the more labor-hours required and the higher the manufacturer's total wage bill. And the more cars made, the more steel used, the more upholstery bought, the more steering wheels ordered, the higher the bill for total materials. Costs in this latter group are called **variable costs** because they fluctuate with output, although the relationship need not be one to one.

In addition, we must realize that the car company has to make a **profit** or go out of business. In a competitive industry and in the long run, the rate of profit for one firm is usually not much higher than for any other, although differences obviously exist.

It seems difficult, however, to classify the auto industry as competitive when one examines the profits of General Motors relative to Ford, Chrysler, and American Motors, or even relative to the average for all manufacturing firms. There have been numerous explanations for GM's rather remarkable capacity to make relatively high profits. One of these involves a phenomenon known as **economies of scale**, or more familiarly, **gains from mass production**. This means that when GM doubles *all* its inputs, its output more than doubles. Thus the larger its production, the smaller its average cost per unit. By producing millions of cars, GM can charge the same price as other companies while clearing higher profits on each car sold. But we are left with a question: Why doesn't GM lower its prices below their present level (for it would still be making a profit) and gradually capture a larger and larger share of the market until no other company exists? We suspect that if GM really enjoys the reputed economies of scale, the reason it fails to do this is the looming potential of an antitrust suit. GM does not want to be broken into bits as was Rockefeller's Standard Oil in 1911.

What, then, determines the price we pay for new cars? In the *short run*, each company will make the most money if it ignores sunk costs (letting bygones be bygones). It should sell cars up to that number at which the revenue from selling an additional automobile will not cover the costs of producing it. The price that gives a company the biggest profits will be about equal to the costs involved in making that hypothetical final car.

We all know, of course, that no carmaker is likely to figure things out by the slide rule of this analytic procedure.[1] We also know, however, that in the *long run* the manufacturer has to cover all costs and earn a "reasonable" profit, or the owners will go into another business where they can make more money.

What, then, is the implication of this latter statement in the matter of required safety features? It is simply that, sooner or later, the costs of such amenities will be paid by the consumer. Seat belts, collapsible steering columns, and dual braking systems require additional resources. Somebody must pay for them, and eventually the tab will be picked up by the buyer of the car, although the manufacturing firm may share the costs if it is earning more than a competitive profit at the outset.

Government regulation of safety features on cars has already raised the price of cars higher than it would have been otherwise.[2] The estimated cost of safety per car is about $450.

Unless the quantity of cars that people demand is totally unresponsive to changes in price, when the price goes up, fewer cars will be bought. Some families will have fewer cars, or will trade in their cars less often, or will depend more on taxis, buses, and trains.

---

[1] We can predict behavior using this theory, though, even if the individual decision-makers do not reason this way.

[2] When **marginal costs** are increased, so, too, is price.

Since imported cars are a substitute for American-made cars, U.S. companies have had every interest in prodding Congress to impose uniform federal safety standards on *all* cars. Otherwise, the relative price of imported automobiles would have fallen and more people would have bought them at the expense, of course, of domestic car sales.

Whether more lives have been or will be saved with the existence of, and compliance with, federal automobile safety standards is, however, a subtle question. When a greater amount of safety is supplied, some individuals will drive less carefully. The economist's standard model will then predict that individuals driving in less safe cars would drive more carefully; individuals driving in safer cars would drive less carefully.

Using such a model, Professor Sam Peltzman has found that there is some empirical support for such predictions because: (1) more than a proportional share of automobile accidents occur with cars that have safety equipment in comparison to those without it, (2) there has been an increased amount of risk taking by drivers, as evidenced by an increase in the amount of drunk driving, and (3) the percentage of auto-related deaths accounted for by pedestrians has increased, relative to those of auto occupants with safety equipment.[3]

We note, for example, that during the period in which safety devices have been required on cars, the number of accidents has increased while the number of deaths of auto occupants has not. These data are again consistent with the view that individuals might be driving more recklessly because of required safety devices on their cars.

Another piece of evidence suggests similar results. A survey of traffic accidents in Texas found that cars weighing less than 3000 pounds accounted for somewhat less than 20 percent of all automobile registrations. The drivers of these cars were involved in 13 percent of the accidents with 16 percent of the injuries. On the other hand, cars that weighed from 4000 to 5000 pounds

[3] Sam Peltzman, "The Regulation of Automobile Safety," in H. G. Manne and R. L. Miller, editors, *Auto Safety Regulations: The Cure of the Problem?* (Horton: Glen Ridge, N.J., 1976).

made up 31 percent of the registrations, but such cars were involved in over 57 percent of the accidents and 51 percent of the injuries. The safer the car, as measured by gross weight, the less cautious the driving habits of the occupant.

Further, even if this risk-taking effect were minimized, we must still realize that safety improvements are not free. Increased safety requires the use of real resources, and thus raises a fundamental issue which cannot be resolved here, but which we should consider. Suppose the new safety standard saves 100, or even 1000, lives a year at an additional price to the consumer of, say, $50 million. Is it worth it? At some price we can make every car a tank so that it will be completely safe for its occupants. Since very few people would care to pay the price of a tank, such an expedient might also solve some problems of pollution and congestion, but it is doubtful that the idea would meet with overwhelming enthusiasm from consumers. In fact, if they were offered a **tradeoff** of various increasing degrees of safety in their cars but at successively higher prices, we would probably find that a great many people would not opt for higher levels of safety. Most would be willing to accept additional risk in trade for a lower-priced automobile.

Note, however, that we have removed this alternative from the consumer. The choice of the price/safety combination that would result from the market forces discussed at the beginning of this chapter has been replaced by a uniform minimum level. The demand for safety has been imposed rather than consumer-derived. Moreover, this minimum level keeps rising as new legislation is passed each year.

Of course, there still exists an argument for imposing safety standards, even if drivers must pay more for their cars. Certain drivers' actions can affect others who have no say in the matter. If a driver has poor brakes, he may run over pedestrians who may never by fully compensated for their injuries. Thus safe brakes are required on all cars. Note, however, that this argument does not apply to padded dashes, for example, which protect only the car's occupants.

We end this chapter by pointing out a current tradeoff that

exists with respect to automobile safety. On one hand, the government is requiring an increasing number of safety products on cars. On the other hand, the government has and continues to require better and better fuel economy. In order to obtain better fuel economy, automobile manufacturers have made smaller and lighter cars. The National Highway Traffic Safety Administration has discovered that if you are in a subcompact car and you collide with a large car, your risk of fatality is 8.2 times greater than the risk for the occupants of the large car. If you are in a mid-size car and you collide with a large car, your risk of fatality is only 1.3 times greater than the risk for the occupants in the large car. Auto insurers are responding accordingly. The State Farm Insurance Company, for example, gives a 15 percent discount for most large cars and imposes a 15 percent surcharge for many small cars. Thus, the tradeoff: To obtain better fuel economy you must assume a greater risk of injury or death if you sustain an accident in a small car.

SUMMARY

Safety is a good. For whatever product it is applied to, safety requires additional cost to the manufacturer and therefore results in a higher price to the consumer. In an unrestricted market, through a trial-and-error system, an array of safety/quality/price options will appear. Some consumers will choose lower-priced, less safe products; others will choose higher-priced, safer products. When safety levels are mandated, as they have been for automobiles, the predicted result is a more reckless use of the product by consumers. Some bits of evidence confirm this hypothesis: Automobiles equipped with safety equipment are involved in a disproportionate share of accidents; there has been an increase in the amount of drunk driving; and a larger percentage of deaths is accounted for by pedestrians. Safety regulations that involve protecting third parties are not subject to the same analysis, however. Thus, some argue against safety regulations relating to padded dashes and collapsible steering wheels, but argue in favor of brake standards, tire standards, and the like.

DISCUSSION QUESTIONS

1. Are there any circumstances under which an automobile manufacturer would want to withhold a safety improvement that required zero additional production costs?
2. Which is more important—fuel economy or automobile safety? Does a choice have to be made between the two?

5

the economics of
Raising Less Corn and More Hell

When Mary Lease stumped the Kansas countryside in 1890, she urged the farmers to raise "less corn and more hell," and that's just what they have been doing ever since.

In the late nineteenth century, their activities took the form of political campaigns aimed toward (1) expanding the **money supply**, which they felt would increase agricultural prices faster than other prices; (2) introducing railroad rate regulation designed to lower freight rates for transporting agricultural products; and (3) curbing monopolies, which they felt would reduce their costs for commodities. When prices of farm goods rose at the start of the twentieth century, the farmers stuck to raising their corn, and during World War I they expanded their production dramatically in response to soaring prices. Then after the war, European countries imposed high taxes on any agricultural goods crossing their borders. Along with other factors, this restriction reduced the amount of corn that American farmers could sell. Farm prices fell sharply in the 1920s and farm organizations began to view their problem as one of relative overproduction. Numerous cooperative efforts were made to restrict production, but these efforts failed (except in the case of a few specialty crops such as tobacco, where the relatively small number of producers made mutual agreement more feasible). Most crops were produced under competitive conditions, that is, a large number of sellers (and buyers) dealt in a product that was undifferentiated (one farmer's corn was just the same as another farmer's corn). Accordingly, it was impossible for producers to organize themselves on a voluntary basis. But what farmers failed to do by voluntary cooperation in the 1920s, they accomplished via governmental directives in the 1930s. A farm **price-support** program was instituted then and was kept intact until a few years ago. We would like to examine the results of the price-support program when it was operative.

We can see the results best by first examining the market for agricultural commodities prior to price supports. In that competitive market, a large number of farmers supplied a commodity —we'll use peanuts as our example. The sum of the quantities that individual farmers will supply at various prices makes up the **aggregate supply** schedule of a commodity. Each farmer supplies only a small part of the aggregate. He cannot influence the price of the product. If he raised his price, anyone wishing to purchase peanuts could easily buy from someone else at the **market-clearing**, or **equilibrium**, **price**. And no farmer would sell below the market-clearing price because he would make less money than possible, since he can sell all that he produces at the market-clearing price. Thus, every unit of output sold by farmers goes for the same price. The price received for the last (*marginal*) unit sold is exactly the same as that received for all the rest.

The farmer will produce peanuts up to the point at which, if one more unit were produced, its production cost would be greater than the price received. Every farmer faces the same production decision. Notice that at higher prices, farmers can incur higher costs for additional units produced and still make a profit; so at higher prices, all farmers together will produce more. But, again, no farmer alone can influence the price. No farmer will stop producing until he stops making a profit. That is, each farmer will end up selling peanuts at the market-clearing price, which will equal his costs of production plus a *normal profit*.[1]

The price at which each farmer can sell his peanuts depends on how people feel about buying them, and that depends on their preferences, incomes, and the prices of substitutes. The demand for food in general is quite unresponsive to price changes because there are no close substitutes for food. The demand for peanuts is more responsive to price changes because of available substitutes. Even so, it takes a drastic reduction in the price of peanuts to get people to buy a lot more. Conversely, an increase in unit price doesn't cause people to buy much less. (The demand for peanuts is relatively *price inelastic*.) This situation has implications for peanut farmers.

Agricultural costs of production and output can vary greatly from year to year because of, among other things, variations in weather. During a good year, production may be relatively large. But since the demand for peanuts is relatively inelastic, farmers will have to reduce drastically the price of their peanut crop if they are to sell it all. They may even have to sustain a loss that year. The opposite situation occurs when production is small one year because of, say, a drought.

In sum, the short-run competitive market in peanuts results in changing prices of the product and changing profits for the producers.

Now how has the usual price-support program worked? The government decided what constituted a "fair price." The formula for this vital determination was the ratio between the prices farmers historically paid for what they bought and the prices they received for their crops in "good" years. How could the

---

[1] This is actually a cost to society, since it is required to keep him farming peanuts instead of changing to an alternative occupation.

government make this arbitrary price "stick" since it was above the level that would have prevailed otherwise?[2] It agreed to buy the peanuts at that (**parity**) price.[3] Actually, the purchase was disguised as a loan from the **Commodity Credit Corporation** that never needed to be repaid. Historically, the government has either stored the peanuts or sold them on the world market (as opposed to the domestic market) at the going price. Since World War II, the world price has often been well below the support price; thus, the government has taken a "loss." For example, in 1976, the support price for nonedible "crushing" peanuts (used for their oil) was $394 per ton, but the world market price was $256 per ton. In effect, then, the U.S. government has been providing **subsidies** to peanut farmers to the tune of $50 to $200 million per year.

In order to prevent too great a surplus, the government in 1941 allowed a maximum of 1.6 million acres to be used for peanut production. However, the yield per acre has tripled since then and the allotments haven't been cut back. Moreover, a large quantity of "illegal" peanuts—peanuts grown on land not officially allowed by the original allotment program—has been grown in the past few years. Since there has been as much as $165 per ton gross profit to be made by selling the peanuts at the support price, it is not surprising that some farmers have wanted to grow peanuts "illegally."

Price supports mean two things, then: (1) higher prices to the consumer for those products whose fixed (parity) price exceeds the price that would otherwise prevail; and (2) more governmental resources (taxpayers' money) expended in agriculture than would otherwise be spent.[4]

If it is true that price supports and acreage restrictions increase the wealth of farmers, there should be every incentive for

[2] Called the market equilibrium price.
[3] This is one possibility only; usually the support price has been between 75 and 90 percent of parity.
[4] Additionally, resources were and are devoted to getting and keeping those subsidy payments; the illegal milk co-op payments exposed during the Watergate investigations are a case in point.

more entrepreneurs to start new farms and to share in the profits. This incipient threat of new competition was met in an interesting way by tobacco farmers. More than three decades ago, they found a way around the problem by fostering legislation which allotted to 500,000 growers the right to raise tobacco on lands then in use. For all practical purposes no new land has been put into production since then, because a prohibitive tax of 75 percent is levied on all tobacco grown on unlicensed land.

Owners of licensed land have thus been granted a **monopoly** in tobacco growing. If you were to buy some of this land today, would you expect to make money as a **monopolist?** If you answered "yes," you are in for a surprise. The price of land was long ago bid up to levels that yield new owners only a competitive rate of return. The ones who made money were the original holders of the tobacco licenses, who reaped profits to the tune of $1500 to $3000 per acre ($4000 to $8000 in current dollars).[5] The same analysis can be made for owners of farmlands after price supports went into effect. One study concluded this: "Most of the net benefit of the price-support program has been capitalized into the value of farmland."[6]

Since the program for controlling tobacco production also includes restrictions on how much leaf each owner can put up for sale and at what price he can sell it, the net results have been: (1) a smaller supply of tobacco than would otherwise have been provided, (2) a higher price for tobacco than would have prevailed under free competition, and (3) a consequent higher price for tobacco products.

The implications of the last statement depend on the **price elasticity of demand** for these products. If people smoke more or less the same quantity of cigarettes and cigars regardless of relatively small variations in price (i.e., if tobacco products face

---

[5] F. H. Maier, J. L. Hendrick, and W. L. Bigson, Jr., *The Sale Value of Flue-Cured Tobacco Allotments,* Agricultural Experiment Station, V.P.I., Technical Bulletin no. 148 (April 1960).

[6] D. Gale Johnson, *Farm Commodity Programs: An Opportunity for Change* (Washington, D.C.: American Enterprise Institute for Public Policy Research, May 1973), p. 3.

elastic demand), then higher prices simply mean that more income will be devoted to tobacco products and less to other things. Since this seems to be the case, the tobacco program has thus resulted in a transfer of income from cigarette smokers to the original owners of the tobacco-growing licenses.

In 1972 and 1973, government officials, concerned laypersons, and many professional economists declared that the world had entered an era of permanent food shortages. Nonetheless, the current farm situation is strikingly similar to what it was during the 1950s and 1960s. That is to say, the government periodically had to get rid of "surplus" butter and cheese. The government had to contend with sugar farmers asking for more restrictions on the amount of imported sugar. The government had to deal with an angry peanut farmers' lobby that did not want price supports cut. By the end of 1981, unsold surplus corn amounted to 50 million metric tons and unsold surplus wheat amounted to over 30 million metric tons. Certainly the notion of a supposed permanent shortage of agricultural products has not prevailed.

SUMMARY

An unrestricted market for farm products yields an equilibrium price at which the quantity demanded equals the quantity supplied. A price support system will lead to an excess quantity supplied if the price support price is above the market-clearing price and if there is some means by which the "surplus" is taken care of. Typically, the government has purchased, in one way or another, "surplus" farm products. Ony when the world price exceeds the price support price do surpluses disappear, as they did in 1973, for example. The lesson to be learned from the history of the agricultural sector is that both consumers and producers respond to disequilibrium situations: Relatively high prices, whether caused by market forces or government intervention, motivate producers to produce more and consumers to consume less.

DISCUSSION QUESTIONS

1. How can there be discussions of permanent food shortages in one year and talk about surpluses in another?
2. There are parts of the world where famines occur. How do such events square with the analysis in this chapter?

the economics of
The Pernambuco Tramway

It sounds plausible. The price of gas, water, oil, electricity, housing, transport—you name it—is too high! So, set a lower price and provide a system of enforcement that prevents chiselers from getting away with illegal prices. Does it work? We might label one attempt the Pernambuco Tramway syndrome, and pass it off as a fairy tale.

Once upon a time, there was a foreign company that received a franchise to build a streetcar system in the growing city of Pernambuco, Brazil. They built the system and people rode back and forth on the streetcars. The original fare (Who can remember way back then?) was one-tenth of a cruzeiro.

It is important to note that the rate was fixed by government edict, and that the foreign company received a return on its investment equal to what it could have obtained with other uses of its funds, or maybe a little higher. (That is, it equaled or exceeded the opportunity cost of the firm's capital.) Now as time went by, the real value of the cruzeiro began to fall because inflation set in. As the beleaguered cruzeiro dropped from a cent to a half-cent to a quarter-cent, the fare—still fixed by edict—no longer produced enough revenue to cover the costs of the system. After a while it could not even cover the costs of current operations (variable costs). The company actually lost money every time a streetcar ran down the street. The company tightened its purse strings; it certainly was not going to put more money into the system. So the cars and rails deteriorated. Every once in a while a loose rail came up through the floorboards and spitted a passenger like a roast pig. Actually, by reducing the quality of service, the tramway operators were raising the real price to users, who now were paying the same fare for a service of dubious value. The streetcars stood empty most of the time. When last heard from, the company was trying to curtail schedules and to sell, or even to give, the operation to the government. This is one fairy tale without a happy ending. But why worry about it?

The reason we worry is that the Pernambuco Tramway syndrome is very much with us. Prices legally held below equilibrium level are a fact of everyday life.

In addition to a gasoline crisis, we face a natural-gas crisis, a garbage-disposal crisis, a water-shortage crisis, and an electricity crisis. While some of these crises also involve other problems, a major factor in each is a price set so low that the amount demanded at that price exceeds the amount suppliers are willing to offer, resulting in a shortage.

In the case of electric power, the consequences are becoming more and more widespread, as indicated by brownouts, blackouts, and sometimes rationing. In some other industries, such as transportation and water systems, the suppliers of electricity face a problem that a single rate exacerbates. The demand for their product at the fixed rate is not constant, but is subject to peak periods. In the case of electricity, the brownouts occur at these periods of extraordinary demand. On the eastern seaboard, for example, the peak demand comes during the hot days of summer when electric air conditioners are whirring. In the Northwest, by contrast, the demand peaks in cold weather as a result of electric space heating. Variations in demand are not only seasonal, but they occur within a day. In some areas the heaviest use comes from 5:00 P.M. to 10:00 P.M., followed by a relatively light demand until 7:00 A.M. In short, we have an industry which has unused capacity for much of the year, and for a good part of every day, but which is strained beyond its capacity for short intervals. To be able to meet these peak demands, the typical electric utility may have to maintain so much excess equipment that it will be operating, on the average, at only 55 percent of capacity.

It is not hard to pinpoint the economics behind the problem. Under a single, uniform rate for electricity, the peak-load user is being subsidized by all other consumers, since the costs of maintaining excess equipment are shouldered equally by all users. If the power company were to adjust the single rate, charging higher prices for peak-period use than for other times, available evidence indicates that less would be demanded at the more costly period. Peak-period use would tend to level off, while the lower price during slack periods would encourage greater use at those times. Skillful planning along such lines might effectively eliminate overloads and their resultant brownouts and blackouts.

Is such an adjustment of the single rate practical? Would it work? It does in France today. Beginning in 1954, *Electricité de France* instituted a tariff pricing system for electricity, with different rates being set to best approximate the actual cost of supplying the additional electricity for any specific season and time of day. Because in the summer months demand is greatest during the day, a higher price is set for the daylight hours than for the night. The differential pricing also takes into account changes in sources of supply. Because winter cuts off the flow of water for hydroelectric stations, more expensive thermal generation must be used. Therefore, French consumers pay more for electricity in winter than in summer. After a careful examination of the French experience, one economist wrote that a "clear improvement over the [old] pricing scheme is very plausibly claimed."[1]

---

[1] Thomas Marschak, "Capital Budgeting and Pricing in the French Nationalized Industries," *Journal of Business* (January 1960), p. 151.

Recently, peak-load pricing for electric utilities in the United States has been strongly proposed by the Environmental Defense Fund (EDF). It was successful in getting the Wisconsin Public Service Commission to implement peak-load pricing for the first time in the United States. The EDF has presented arguments for peak-load pricing not only in Wisconsin but also in New York, Michigan, California, and elsewhere.

SUMMARY

Companies that provide transportation service will provide the same quality of service only as long as they make a normal rate of return to their investment. If a price control is imposed that effectively reduces the transportation company's rate of return to investment, the company will allow quality to decrease such that the price per constant quality unit will remain the same. The same is true for companies providing electricity services. If not allowed to charge a price that yields investors a normal rate of return, quality will decrease. One way to improve the pricing system of electricity is to charge higher prices during peak periods; this is called peak-load pricing and it is being used in certain utility districts in the United States apparently with some success.

DISCUSSION QUESTIONS

1. What do we mean when we say that a reduction in quality raises the price per constant quality unit?
2. How could peak-load pricing reduce the potential of brownouts and blackouts?

7

the economics of
Wage and Price Controls

What happens when you don't let the price system work? That's not an idle question. Ever since the time of the Roman Emperor Diocletian, the response of government to rising prices has been to impose a ceiling on prices and wages. As recently as 1971 President Nixon imposed such wage and price controls. Even after what was widely perceived by economists as the disastrous consequence of these controls and their elimination in 1974, a Gallup poll in November of that year showed that 62 percent of the American people favored them. As of this writing they are an ever-present possibility.

The answer to the question posed in the first sentence is that you can't prevent the price system from working in one way or another. But you can make it work so inefficiently that it may produce horrendous costs to the system, arbitrarily punish some and reward others, and, in the extreme, lead to the complete breakdown of the system itself. In order to understand this, we must understand a little more about the nature of goods and services and the way in which they are transacted. It is a useful simplification to think of economic transactions as involving the instantaneous exchange of a unidimensional good for a sum of money (e.g., paying 50 cents for a loaf of bread). But goods are not unidimensional; they are composed of a large number of different characteristics of differing qualities. Consider the loaf of bread, for example. Bread is made up of a number of ingredients. The baker, in the face of rising costs and a price ceiling, has the option of reducing the size of the loaf of bread, or reducing the quality of the flour or the quantity and quality of other inputs. Bread, however, is a relatively simple commodity as compared to, say, an automobile. In the face of price ceilings, the automobile producer likewise has literally thousands of options to alter the quality of the automobile.

Note the implications of this point. A reduction in quality at a constant price enforced by a price ceiling is, in fact, a price increase since what we have is an inferior automobile at the same price as before. But we have only begun to contemplate the impossible task that faces the administrator of price ceilings. What about seasonal variations in the real cost of providing goods? Should the price of lettuce in midwinter be the same as the price of lettuce in summer? If it is, we can be assured that the lettuce will disappear in midwinter if the summer price is imposed. And if we impose the winter price of lettuce, then we are giving windfall gains to summer lettuce producers. What about the goods that we import in international competition? Do we impose a price ceiling on them? If we do and their prices rise, it simply means that we will no longer be able to import them. This will lead to shortages, which in turn will prevent production or raise the cost to other producers who use those goods as inputs into their manufacturing.

It should be clear from the foregoing that an efficient price control system is simply impossible. However, the problem is even more complex because some prices are much easier to force a ceiling upon than others. The number of goods and services required to enforce a wage or price ceiling is staggering to contemplate. There are literally hundreds of millions of individual goods and services for which the administrator must devise and enforce a ceiling. Wages, for example, are very visible; they exist in contracts, and therefore a wage ceiling is much easier to enforce than is a price ceiling when changes in quality are made. The result is that certain kinds of prices will be effectively enforced while others, in fact, will change. As a consequence, we can have an immense real redistribution of income in the system, favoring those who can circumvent price ceilings and injuring those whose products or services can be easily and effectively regulated.

We have already observed two major dilemmas of wage and price fixing. First, hidden changes in quality and other adjustments will in fact lead to disguised but real price increases in many parts of the system and to an inability to control prices in others. Second, arbitrary redistribution of wealth and income penalizes some and favors others. But by all odds, the most serious consequence is that wage and price controls do not enable the market to perform its primary task, which is to act as a self-adjusting mechanism that resolves problems of changes in supply and demand over a period of time.

What makes the market system efficient is that prices serve as signals which, in turn, lead to alterations in the behavior of suppliers on the one hand and buyers on the other. Thus, when prices of a commodity are going up, they reflect the fact that demand is increasing relative to supply. In consequence, suppliers realize it would be more profitable to invest more in producing more of that good. In turn, supply expands relative to demand, and a fall in price results. Thus, without anyone having issued commands, the price system has produced a set of results that have resolved the dilemma arising from short-run disequilibrium between supply and demand. Where the price system is not allowed to work, we observe that shortages become permanent, because the price ceiling prevents the signaling process from working by making it unprofitable for suppliers to adjust output in the face of changing demands for their goods and services. The history of rent control in New York City is perhaps the most famous modern example. It has led not only to the **rationing** of the supply of apartments available, but, also to a failure of suppliers of buildings to build new apartments. This has resulted in a chronic and perpetual shortage of apartments in New York City. We treat this important phenomenon in more detail in Chapter 18. But rent control has more serious consequences: The tax base of New York has been primarily based upon housing real estate and as its tax base has eroded, the fiscal income of the city has declined. The consequences of that decline are with us today as New York struggles to extricate itself from thirty-five years of rent control.

The overall economic consequences of wage and price controls are disastrous, but their continued popularity with the public suggests that our analysis is incomplete. There are those who benefit from such controls. If you were already renting an apartment in New York City, you gained—at least in the short run. And, as in the example of an overall wage and price freeze described in the beginning of this chapter, we can see that there are many groups that can evade the controls—and they are winners too. Finally, it is clear that a great many people simply do not understand the long-run implications of such controls. It is appealing to have a law that says you won't have to pay more for goods and services, but it is not easy to understand the way markets operate. The political economy of wage and price controls is a much more intractable issue than its simple economics would suggest.

SUMMARY

Wage and price controls, when effective, create shortages and reductions in quality. To be effective, a wage or price control must be set below the market-clearing price, or wage rate. There must also be an enforcement mechanism to prevent avoidance or evasion of the controls. But since there are literally trillions of transactions undertaken every year in the United States, it is virtually impossible for any enforcement mechanism to be completely successful when, in fact, the forces of supply and demand dictate a market-clearing price, or wage, that is above the controlled price or wage. The existence of wage and price controls eliminates or, at a minimum, attenuates the signaling aspect of prices in a market system.

DISCUSSION QUESTIONS

1. If wage and price controls have the pernicious effects outlined in this chapter, why are they so popular?
2. Suppose that a control is imposed on the price of gasoline at the pump. In what ways can customers and gas station owners alike avoid or evade that control?

8

the economics of
Water

Not a year goes by without some area of the country suffering a water problem or even a water crisis. A typical headline is "Water is in Permanent Short Supply in Some Parts of the Country and Getting That Way in Others."[1]

One winter at the beginning of this decade, New York City had only four months' supply of water, and government officials permitted restaurants to serve water only if customers asked for it. The Mississippi River has often been too shallow to float barge and tow boat traffic. Even southern Florida, where in the rainy season torrential rains pummel the land day after day, has had sporadic water problems.

Water is a problem, of that there is no doubt. But is the problem that we are running out of water, as a *Newsweek* headline

[1] *Changing Times*, July 1981, p. 33.

once asked? The common view of water is that it is a precious **resource** that is being overused and yes, indeed, we are running out of it. The economic analysis of the water problem, however, is not quite so pessimistic nor so tied to the physical quantities of water that exist on our earth and in the atmosphere. Rather, an economic analysis of water follows along lines similar to an analysis of any other scarce resource.

The water industry is one of the oldest and largest in the United States. The philosophy surrounding the water industry merits some analysis. Many commentators believe that water is unique, that it should not be treated as an **economic good**, that is, a scarce good. Engineering studies that concern themselves with demand for residential water typically use a "requirements" approach. The forecaster simply predicts population changes and then multiplies those estimates by the currently available data showing the average amount of water used per person. The underlying assumption for such a forecast is that regardless of the price charged for water in the future, the same quantity will be demanded. Implicitly, then, both the short- and long-run price elasticities of demand are assumed to be zero.

Many residential water systems charge a flat monthly rate. Each household pays a specified amount of dollars per month no matter how much water is used. This was the case in Boulder, Colorado, prior to 1961.

An alternative approach to determining payment for water involves using meters at each residence. In 1961, in Boulder, Colorado, the water utility installed water meters in every home (and business) that it supplied. Each residence was charged 35 cents per thousand gallons of water used. In essence, the flat fee charged before 1961 meant that a zero price was being charged at the margin (for any incremental use of water). The introduction of a usage meant that a positive price for the marginal unit of water was now imposed.

Economist Steve Hanke looked at the quantity of water demanded both before and after the meters were installed in Boulder, Colorado.[2] Hanke first developed what he calls the "ideal" use of water for each month throughout the year. He completed his "ideal" use estimates by taking account of the average irrigable area per residence, the average temperature during the month, the average number of daylight hours, and the effect of rainfall. The term *ideal* implies nothing from an economic point of view, merely indicating the minimum quantity of sprinkling water required to maintain the aesthetic quality of each residence's lawn.

From the data in Table 8-1, which compares water usage in Boulder with and without metering, we find that individuals sprinkled their lawns much more under the flat-rate system than they did under the metered-rate system. The data presented in column 3 of the table are for the one-year period after the metering system was put into effect.

TABLE 8-1   Comparing Water Usage with and without Metering of Actual Usage

(1) Meter Routes	(2) Actual Sprinkling to Ideal Sprinkling, Flat Rate Period	(3) Actual Sprinkling to Ideal Sprinkling, Metered Rate Period
16, 18	128	78
37	175	72
53, 54	156	72
70, 71, 72	177	63
73, 75	175	97
74	175	102
76, 78	176	105
79	157	86

Source: Steve Hanke, "Demand for Water under Dynamic Conditions," *Water Resources Research,* vol. 6, no. 5 (October 1970).

[2] "Demand for Water under Dynamic Conditions," *Water Resources Research,* vol. 6, no. 5 (October 1970), pp. 1253–1261.

Column 1 shows the meter route numbers arbitrarily assigned by the municipality. Column 2 shows how much water was used in the different routes during the period when a flat rate was charged for water usage. It is expressed in terms of actual sprinkling compared to "ideal" sprinkling. In column 3, actual sprinkling is compared to "ideal" sprinkling, but under a system of metered-rate pricing in which each user is charged for the actual amount of water used. Hanke's data indicate that the quantity of water demanded is a function of the price charged for water. Moreover, Hanke found that for many years after the imposition of the metered-rate pricing system for water, the quantity of water demanded not only remained at a lower level than before metering, but continued to fall slightly. That, of course, means that the long-run price elasticity of demand for water was greater than the short-run price elasticity of demand.

The water issue threatens to become the major issue of the 1980s and 1990s. In many parts of the country, water is either treated as **common property**, in which no one has clear-cut ownership rights, or it is sold by municipal water systems that refuse to charge a market-clearing price. That is not to say that solving water "shortages" is easy or without cost. To the extent that communities do not currently have water metering systems (they charge a flat rate per month), resources will have to be expended to install metering systems. Also, for farming areas where wells can be drilled into a common water table, it will be costly and perhaps difficult to monitor farmers' use of water for irrigation. However, the fact that resources must be spent to meter and charge for water ultimately will not deter communities from implementing a metered-rate system. This is so because after a certain point, regardless of any one's philosophy about water, some form of pricing will have to be instituted that reduces the quantity demanded to equal the quantity supplied. In the long run, economics has a way of influencing even those political decision makers who refuse to admit the need for market pricing to solve resource crises.

SUMMARY

Numerous water shortages appear throughout the United States on a regular basis. These water shortages are typically blamed on lack of rain or excessive use of the resource. However, an economist will argue that water shortages only exist because of an improper pricing system in which individuals are not forced to pay the full social opportunity cost of the water used. At least one study has shown that, at a higher price for water, the demand can be decreased dramatically. Water that is treated as common property or owned by a municipality and sold at a flat fee per month will ultimately have to be rationed, by price, to make the quantity demanded just equal the quantity supplied and thereby eliminate periodic shortages.

DISCUSSION QUESTIONS

1. In your opinion, do the data presented in Table 8-1 refute the "water is different" philosophy?
2. If the price elasticity of demand for water in the short run and in the long run were equal, what would you expect to happen to the quantity of water demanded after a price increase?
3. Do the data from Boulder, Colorado, give any indication about how water shortages can be solved?

part two
Market Structures

INTRODUCTION

Markets can take on many forms. The standard market structures that are usually discussed are (1) pure competition, (2) **monopolistic competition,** (3) **oligopoly,** and (4) monopoly. In this part, examples of these market structures are given.

An example of the perfectly competitive market is the market for publicly traded shares of **common stock.** It can be argued that such a market is extremely efficient, with the result that it is extremely difficult to "make a killing" by trading in that market, particularly if one uses **public information.** The monopolistically competitive market structure is illustrated by the economics of cents-off coupons. It is argued that retail food outlets are able to use price discrimination by means of cents-off coupons. Only in a situation of less-than-perfect competition could such price discrimination occur. And only in a world of less-than-perfect competition will advertising occur, which is the subject matter of another chapter. The worlds of oligopoly and monopoly are illustrated by an analysis of ethical drug regulation, the medical industry, and international cartels.

One point should be kept in mind throughout this part: We are presenting models of human behavior, not of thought processes. Our analysis of the medical profession, for example cannot be proved or disproved by asking physicians whether they think along the lines of our analysis. Our models are set up using an "as if" type of framework. That is to say, we assume that the individuals under study are acting as if they are attempting to maximize their own self-interest.

the economics of
Drug Regulation

Medical drugs are a two-edged sword. If they are carefully manufactured, appropriate for curing your illness, and free of side
effects, your pain and suffering may be prevented, or at least as-
suaged. If, on the other hand, the drug you happen to take under
your doctor's supervision turns out to have side effects, you may
be worse off than if you had never taken the drug at all, or taken
an alternative drug without side effects. Federal regulation has
been concerned not only with the safety, but also with the efficacy—the effectiveness—of drugs for many years. The first
federal legislation, the Food and Drug Act of 1906, dealt with
adulteration and misbranding. Safety was also covered under the
adulteration section. That act prohibited inclusion of any substance that would be poisonous or harmful to health. To some extent, the act was successful. Dr. Hostetter's celebrated Stomach
Bitters and Kickapoo Indian Sagwa, along with numerous rum-

laden concoctions and anticancer remedies, disappeared from the alchemists' shelves as a result of this legislation. The original act was expanded in 1938 with the passage of the Federal Food, Drug, and Cosmetic Act, which forced manufacturers to demonstrate the safety of new drugs. It resulted from public reaction to the deaths of about 75 individuals who had taken an elixir of sulfanilamide. This was the chemical compound sulfanilamide dissolved in diethylene glycol, which is a poisonous substance usually used as antifreeze.

The next big public outrage came after the birth of numerous deformed infants whose mothers had been taking a sleeping pill called Thalidomide. At the time that these deformities were publicized, the Food and Drug Administration (FDA) was actually moving toward approving Thalidomide in the United States. About two-and-a-half million Thalidomide tablets were in the hands of physicians as samples. At the insistence of President John F. Kennedy, the FDA removed all of the samples. Using the Thalidomide scandal as ammunition, Senator Estes Kefauver secured passage of his bill, known as the 1962 Kefauver-Harris Amendments to the 1938 Food, Drug, and Cosmetic Act. Kefauver and his associates wished to prevent, among other things, a proliferation of new drugs. Prior to the 1962 amendments, the FDA normally approved a new drug application within 180 days, unless the application did not adequately demonstrate during that time that the drug was safe for use as suggested in the proposed labeling. The 1962 amendments added a "proof of efficacy" requirement and removed the time constraint on the FDA. Thus, since 1962, no drug can be marketed unless and until the FDA determines that it is safe and effective in its intended use.

Let's reiterate here what is at issue. Legislation has been passed and the FDA enforces it so that two things are prevented: (1) the marketing of unsafe drugs, and (2) the proliferation of drugs that are "unnecessary" in the sense that similar efficacy could be obtained by older, already tested drugs. Consumers presumably are better protected by this legislation because generally they do not have the ability to obtain (let alone fully analyze) the information necessary to make an accurate choice about the safety or efficacy of a particular drug. They are, in a sense, at the mercy of their physicians. But their physicians are also, in a sense, at the mercy of the drug companies. Physicians cannot possibly keep up with the technical literature about drugs and comprehend the differences among them. To keep the medical profession informed, drug companies spend thousands of dollars a year per physician. They send out so-called detail men to inform physicians of new drugs and to give them samples to dispense to patients, so doctors can find out for themselves how effective the drugs really are. To be sure, doctors, hospitals, and drug companies do have an incentive to prescribe, market, and produce safe drugs. After all, if it can be proven that side effects from drug use cause harm to an individual, the ensuing lawsuit will certainly make the doctor, hospital, and/or manufacturer worse off. Additionally, the negative publicity surrounding such a lawsuit will not enhance the future reputation of the drug company involved. And, finally, the more lawsuits filed and won by injured parties, the higher the total cost of production of drugs, and the higher the price ultimately paid by the consumer. Assuming there is at least some price elasticity of demand for drugs (that it is not zero), the resultant higher price to the consumer will cause a reduction in the quantity demanded.

The 1962 amendments seem to have been very effective, given that the number of new drugs introduced into the medical marketplace has been drastically reduced. From 1961 to 1962, the number of new chemical entities and new drugs introduced was about 340. From 1963 to 1970, when the Kefauver Amendments were in effect, the number dropped to an average of 110 annually. That should not be surprising. The cost of introducing a new drug has risen dramatically. Prior to the 1962 amendments, the average time between filing and approval of a new drug application was 7 months; by 1967, it was 30 months. In other words, the 1962 amendments have added at least two years to the period during which new drugs must be continuously tested. In making investment decisions, firms are keenly aware of this additional cost.

The effect of such costs has been what some people call the

U.S. drug lag. For example, in 1976 the number of new and important chemical entities introduced for the first time was 39 in Germany, 38 in France, 23 in Italy, and 15 in the United States. The number of drugs marketed in England which are not available in the United States is very much larger than the reverse situation. Consequently, increasing numbers of individuals in the United States seek medical care abroad. Individuals are sending their children to England to obtain sodium valproate, the only known medicine that can control certain epileptic seizures in young children. Heart specialists contend that they are severely restricted by the FDA because they cannot prescribe a whole range of so-called beta blockers to help protect coronary patients against heartbeat irregularities and potentially fatal heart attacks. The FDA so far has approved only two beta blockers, whereas there are nine such drugs in Britain.

Now we come to the realization that for every benefit, there seems to be a cost. Clearly, there is a dollar cost to the drug companies in testing more completely the efficacy and safety of a drug. But if that were the only issue, there probably wouldn't be many critics of the FDA. The reason there are so many critics today is the cost to individuals, who might be better off if more drugs had been introduced into the United States since 1962.

Let's now consider the safety problem in total. Every time a new drug is introduced, it has potentially harmful side effects. Thus, part of the cost of introducing that drug is the cost of the undesired side effects to those who incur them. This is called a "Type I error." It is the probability of being wrong; that is, of having introduced a drug that should not have been introduced. Since 1962, we have reduced the Type I error—the Thalidomide possibility—by increasing the amount of testing necessary for the introduction of new drugs. People have undoubtedly benefited by this reduction in Type I error by incurring fewer side effects. But other people have been hurt. They have been the victims of what is called a "Type II error." Their cost is the pain, suffering, and possible death that occur because of the lack of availability of a drug that *would have been offered* on the marketplace in the absence of the 1962 amendments. The Type II error, then, is the probability of not introducing new drugs that should have been introduced. To understand better the cost of a Type I error, consider the possibility of the 1962 drug amendments being applied to aspirin. It is very hard to demonstrate *why* aspirin is effective—and it may have bad side effects—such as duodenal ulcers—if taken often. Imagine, though, if it had never been introduced. What would the cost have been? People would have incurred more pain from headaches, arthritis, and so on. In other words, the Type II error cost is the pain and suffering that occur because a drug was *not* introduced.

The public is very much aware of Type I errors. Thalidomide scandals make big news. It is very hard to estimate Type II error costs, however. Only recently have doctors started speaking out against the FDA regulations that limit the introduction of new drugs into the United States. When they must send their patients to England or Canada or Mexico to get drugs, it becomes clear to them that their patients are paying a cost because of stringent FDA regulations.

Does that mean that we should eliminate the FDA altogether? Certainly not. In order to assess the effectiveness of any policy, we must look at both the costs and the benefits. The costs of Type II errors are very hard to assess. We have to come up with an estimate of the kinds of drugs that would have been developed and then further estimate the value that people would have placed on their reduced suffering from the introduction of such drugs. Sam Peltzman, an economist, has attempted to do such a study and his results are as follows:

> The 1962 Drug Amendments sought to reduce consumer waste on ineffective drugs. This goal appears to have been obtained, but the cost in the process seemed clearly to have outweighed the benefits. It was shown (in this study) that the Amendments have produced a substantial decline in innovations since 1962. . . . The net effect of the Amendments on consumers, then, is comparable to their being taxed something between 5 and 10 percent on their . . . drug purchases.[1]

[1] Sam Peltzman, "An Evaluation of Consumer Protection Legislation: The 1962 Drug Amendments," *Journal of Political Economy*, vol. 81 (September/October, 1972), pp. 1089–1090.

Peltzman's study is, of course, not definitive, particularly since he had to use many approximations of the value of human life, the cost of suffering, and so on. But he does make us rethink the true costs of an economic action, and his study can be applied to many other policy issues in the economy. Whenever we reduce the number of accidents related to the use of a product or service, we necessarily must reduce the level of benefits received from using that product or service by a certain group of individuals. In other words, when a product is made safer, a cost is usually involved that raises the price of the product. Individuals who would have used that product had it not been for the price increase may be worse off; individuals who use the product and suffer fewer harmful effects from so doing are better off.

SUMMARY

The regulation of the ethical drug market has had long-run effects. It is impossible to reduce the probability of undesired side effects from new drugs without increasing the probability that fewer beneficial drugs will be available to help those who need them. In statistical terms, this is called the tradeoff between a Type I and Type II error. In a world of **scarce resources**, this tradeoff always exists. If we wanted to eliminate all Type I errors —that is, all negative side effects—we could make all ethical drugs illegal. But the cost in terms of Type II errors—the loss of all the drugs that help alleviate pain and suffering, and postpone death—would be enormous.

DISCUSSION QUESTIONS

1. Does the type of market structure in which drugs are produced have anything to do with the tradeoff between Type I and Type II errors? In other words, would our analysis be different if the drug industry were either perfectly competitive or a pure monopoly?

2. Apply the analysis of Type I and Type II errors to the adjustment of headlights on automobiles. (Hint: a Type I error would involve adjusting the headlights too high so as to seriously impair the vision of oncoming drivers.)

10

the economics of
Rising
Medical Costs

Most people don't have to be told about how expensive it is these days to see a doctor or to go into a hospital. If we compare the **Consumer Price Index** with a medical care price index, we see that since 1950 the CPI has increased by 280 percent, while the medical care index has increased by 350 percent. We spent only $4 billion on medical care in 1929; we increased our spending to $40 billion by 1965; and today it is over $250 billion. In 1929, expenditures on medical care represented only 4 percent of total national spending, but today's expenditures represent 10 percent. We can say, therefore, that as real income rises, Americans demand not just more medical care, but more in proportion to their rising incomes.[1]

If we wish to understand why medical care is so expensive, we have to look at a number of factors. They include (1) past

---

[1] In other words, the **income elasticity of demand** for medical care exceeds 1.

restrictions on the supply of physicians, (2) increases in demand created by Medicare and Medicaid, (3) increases in the quantity of care demanded due to third-party insurance, and (4) soaring medical malpractice insurance costs and resultant increases in so-called defensive medicine.

Entry into the medical profession is by no means unrestricted. Latest figures show, for example, that about 75,000 people take the standard medical school admissions test and only 13,000 are accepted. The number of applicants to Harvard's medical school runs to almost 3500, but the class size remains at less than 150. Some students apply to as many as 10 different medical schools and when turned down, reapply two or three times. The number of students who don't apply because they know the odds are so much against them is probably two or three times the number of those who take the chance. Moreover, many applicants don't get into medical school because the number of medical schools in the United States is severely restricted.

In principle, they are restricted as a result of state licensing requirements, which universally prohibit proprietary medical schools (schools run for profit). A medical school must be accredited by the state for its graduates to be allowed to take the licensing exam required for practicing medicine. If we look back to the first decade of this century, we find that there were 192 medical schools in the United States. By 1944, that number had declined to 69. The number of physicians per 100,000 people dropped from 157 in 1900 to 132 in 1957. The reason for these precipitous declines was the success of the American Medical Association in controlling the output of doctors.

The regulation and certification of medical schools were based on the findings of the so-called Flexner Report. In 1910, the prestigious Carnegie Foundation commissioned Abraham Flexner[2] to inspect the existing medical education facilities in the United States. Flexner's recommendations resulted in the demise

---

[2] Flexner was a historian whose brother was the Johns Hopkins University medical dean. The model Flexner used to judge the "quality" of all other medical schools was the medical school at Johns Hopkins.

of half of the then-existing medical schools.[3] It is interesting to note that Flexner (himself not a physician or even a scientist) was examining the *inputs* and not the *outputs* of the schools. Instead of finding out how well or how qualified the *graduates* of the different schools were, he looked at how they were taught. This is equivalent to your instructor giving you a grade on the basis of how many hours you spent studying rather than how well you did on the final exam.

The purpose of the stricture on medical schools was described by the former head of the AMA's Council on Medical Education, who said in 1928 that

> the reduction of the number of medical schools from 160 to 80 (resulted in) a marked reduction in number of medical students and medical graduates. We had anticipated this and felt that this was a desirable thing. We had . . . a great oversupply of poor and mediocre practitioners.

In economic terms, the supply curve shifted inward as the demand curve either remained stable or shifted outward. The result was that the price of physicians' services went up, thereby allowing them to make higher incomes. The census of 1970, for example, showed that physicians had the highest income of any profession.[4] In that year, it was on average $41,500, at a time when self-employed dentists earned $28,100, engineers $17,700, and college full professors $16,800. In 1974, the median net income of physicians who incorporated themselves was $72,500.

We can ask ourselves whether the AMA's avowed wishes were satisfied. The AMA maintained that the qualifications of many doctors were deficient—that the public was being serviced by doctors who were doing damage to unsuspecting patients. The idea behind medical school licensing was to weed out the most unqualified students and to eliminate the possibility of an unsus-

---

[3] Some medical historians believe that before 1900, doctors probably killed more people than they cured. The Carnegie Foundation and the American Medical Association certainly had legitimate concerns about the quality of medical care at that time.

[4] Part of this is due, however, to longer average hours worked per week.

pecting sick person being treated by an inadequately trained, yet licensed, doctor. It is strange, though, that the AMA did not seek in 1910 to analyze the qualifications of the current crop of physicians. The closure of one-half of the medical schools resulted in the elimination of the *future* supply of supposedly unqualified doctors, but the supposedly unqualified doctors who were already in practice were allowed to continue practicing until retirement or death. Additionally, it would seem that the AMA would wish doctors, even after attending a qualified medical school, to be reexamined periodically in order to continue practicing.

It is possible, too, that the *quality* of medical care consumed by the public did not increase as much as the AMA professed it did after the closure of half of the medical schools. After all, there are two kinds of medical services. One is self-diagnosis and self-treatment; the other is relying on someone in the medical care industry. If the price of a physician's diagnosis and treatment goes up, then one might expect that the quantity demanded would fall, and an increased reliance on self-diagnosis and self-treatment would result. People would go to doctors only after their symptoms became alarming. It may be, then, that the increase in the quality—and therefore the price—of doctors' services resulted in a *decrease* in the *total* quality of medical care utilized, because doctors were consulted less often. Moreover, when the price of the services of licensed physicians goes up, there is an increase in the demand for substitute healing services, and these substitutes may well be inferior to even a poorly trained M.D.

Concurrently with the restriction on the supply of physicians in the United States, there have been, at times, dramatic increases in demand, which have brought about rising prices. Certain government programs have shifted the demand curve to the right. One of these programs is Medicare, free medical care for the aged. Prior to Medicare, congressional estimates of what that program would cost were many times less than what the actual cost turned out to be. This can be easily explained, since the demand for medical services is responsive to the price charged. When Medicare was instituted, the actual price of health care services to many people was drastically lowered, and in some cases, reduced to zero. As the price fell, the quantity demanded rose — so much so that the available supply of medical services was taxed beyond capacity. The only thing that could give was the price, and it gave. Hospital room charges have skyrocketed since the imposition of Medicare and its state counterpart, Medicaid.[5]

Similar in their effects are medical insurance plans rooted in the private sector of the economy. At least 90 million Americans are covered by some private medical insurance. Generally this insurance pays a percentage of hospital expenses. Herein lies a problem: insurance usually covers inpatient services, rarely outpatient services. Individuals covered by insurance therefore have an incentive to go to a hospital to be taken care of by their private doctors, and their private doctors have an incentive to send them there in order to collect payment. And as with Medicare and Medicaid, private insurance plans increase the quantity of services demanded simply because the direct out-of-pocket costs are very low or zero. The insurance industry has a term for this — moral hazard. In economics, we translate this term to state that the demand curve slopes down (i.e., that the quantity of services demanded increases when the price falls).[6] Many medical services could be postponed or never used at all; for example, cosmetic surgery and, to a lesser extent, other elective surgery. But the lower the price charged, the more cosmetic and elective surgery will be undertaken. And the lower the price, the more likely people are to visit their doctors when they have a slight ailment, such as a cold. In other words, when people are directly charged the full price of their physicians' services, they are likely to use them more sparingly. But if the price is reduced to practically zero, some of them (at least those on the margin) will respond by seeing their physicians for minor ailments.

Furthermore, due to third-party insurance and Medicare

[5] Doctors now order just as many expensive tests for their poor Medicare patients as they do for their rich patients.

[6] Of course, the full price, including the insurance premium, does not fall — it rises. But the insurance premium is a fixed cost. It does not vary with the number of visits to the doctor or trips to the hospital.

and Medicaid, doctors, in conjunction with hospitals, have been ordering more and more tests, using more and more advanced techniques. Hospitals have an incentive to use the most exotic techniques possible and doctors to order them, knowing full well that patients will be reimbursed by their insurance companies for a large percentage of the cost. The problem is that patients covered by insurance do not pay the *direct* cost of the medical care they receive in a hospital at the time they receive it. Obviously, they pay eventually through higher premiums, but that cost is spread out over everyone who buys the insurance. The result is that the quantity of services demanded in the hospital will be more than it otherwise would be. This causes hospital expenses to go up, all other things held constant.

The above discussion gives some idea of what might happen if we had a fully comprehensive national health insurance program. National health insurance is not a different way to provide medical services, just a different way to pay for them. Insurance for everyone does nothing about the supply of insurance. Its chief benefit will be to make sure that the medical services an individual obtains will be paid for by a national insurance plan. The plan, however, has to be paid for by someone. The full opportunity cost of medical services will be paid by all the people in the United States, in one way or another. At the writing of this edition, national health insurance has not yet become a reality for all Americans, although bills have been proposed in Congress for many years. One of the most far-reaching has been identified with Senator Edward M. Kennedy of Massachusetts. In its first form Kennedy's National Security Act would have been a completely public program financed by employer and employee payments to a trust fund modeled on the social security system. There would have been virtually no deductible clause, that is to say, all Americans would have been able to get virtually all medical care without any direct payment. The effect of having no deductible amount would have been to dramatically increase the quantity of medical care services demanded. We know this to be a fact, given the big changes in the demand for medical care by people over 65 after the introduction of Medicare. It has been suggested that one way to solve this problem is to include in any national health care plan a deductible of, say, $500 per family. Each family would have to pay the $500 of medical care services before national health insurance took over. In this matter, families on the margin would think twice about going to visit the family doctor for a simple cold.

We cannot avoid the medical care cost problem by having "free medical care" on the British model, as some individuals believe. Free medical care does not exist even in Britain. The British merely pay for it indirectly, through drains on general tax revenues, instead of directly, by individual patients settling accounts with individual doctors. The United States could socialize medicine, but we would still have to pay the opportunity cost of all services received. If the supply of doctors were still controlled by the AMA and the government regulated their pay scales, we might end up with *less* medical care than now, for there would be even fewer doctors than at present. This last statement does not constitute an argument against socialized medicine. With adequate salary incentives, we could have as many doctors as required. Socialization of medicine, in fact, allows low-income people (actually *all* people) to obtain needed medical care for which they might not choose to spend their money if they were forced to pay for it directly. More people would be induced to seek medical care because the cost would be borne indirectly by the whole community instead of by individuals. If society feels this is a desirable goal, then socialization of medicine is a possible way of achieving it.

Medical malpractice insurance increases have been in the news for several years now. Individuals are suing their doctors and hospitals more than ever before, and juries are awarding them ever-larger amounts. The result? Skyrocketing malpractice insurance costs.

Let's look at a few examples. In 1972 Baylor University Medical Center in Dallas, Texas, paid $11,000 for malpractice insurance; in 1976, the bill was $1.5 million. In 1974, Mt. Sinai Hospital Medical Center in Chicago paid $281,000 for $6 million in malpractice insurance; in 1976, the same insurance companies wanted $3 million to provide the same coverage. Had the hospital paid the premium sought by the insurance companies, the cost of malpractice insurance to the patient would have gone up from $7 to $22 per day.

Former Attorney General Griffin B. Bell has indicated that throughout the United States "malpractice costs by themselves add approximately $5 per day to every person who requires hospitalization." That is six times what it was a few years ago.

A number of hospitals have stopped paying regular insurance companies for such coverage. Instead, they are self-insuring; that is, they set aside a certain sum of money each month in a reserve account to cover any claims against them in malpractice lawsuits. Unfortunately, this means that some hospitals could conceivably go out of business if an extraordinarily large malpractice suit was won by a former patient.

The increased possibility of being sued has caused doctors to engage in what is known as defensive medicine. Defensive medicine involves ordering many more tests, for example, than doctors would normally order, just to cover themselves in case of a lawsuit. Reasonable and standard care in medicine now includes many more blood tests and x-rays, and more consultations with other specialists than in the past. Of course, someone has to pay for this defensive medicine, and that someone is either the taxpayer, through Medicaid or Medicare, the subscriber to a private medical insurance plan, or the patient directly.

Some concerned individuals have suggested that the government step in to offer malpractice insurance to hospitals that do not feel they can "afford" the now higher rates. This would mean, however, that hospitals could then force the general taxpayer to cover any of their mistakes. In 1979, the Justice Department proposed a sweeping court reform plan aimed directly at holding down the cost of medical malpractice insurance. The Justice Department wants the states to set up screening panels that will filter all malpractice suits before they come to trial. Presumably such a system would weed out unfounded claims and encourage prompt settlement of those that have merit. (Actually, about half the states have similar laws on the books, but the constitutionality of such screening panels has already been challenged.) In the future, there may be other solutions to the malpractice insurance problem, but today it remains a problem.

We end this chapter with a discussion about the future supply of medical care personnel. No longer can we say that there is a shortage of physicians in the United States. Recent rates of medical school graduates and the addition of foreign-trained physicians who are immigrating to the United States will eliminate—or have already eliminated—this "shortage." In addition, Congress has enacted a number of bills to increase the supply of medical personnel. For example, in 1971 the Comprehensive Manpower Training Act and the Nurse Training Act were passed. At the beginning of 1970, there were already predictions of "excess capacity" in medical schools and a "surplus" of physicians by the mid 1980s. The AMA takes this line, and it is not hard to understand why. Current data show that since 1970, physicians' earnings may not have kept pace with increases in the cost of living. Undoubtedly, that is due to the larger number of physicians entering practice. The obvious way to change this situation is to reduce future increases in the supply of physicians. The growth rate of M.D.s in the United States is now 3.8 percent a year, which is far greater than the population growth rate of 0.8 percent a year. Today, there are 177 doctors per 100,000 people. By 1990, given current rates, there will be 232 per 100,000 people.

This increase in the supply of doctors has been noted with alarm by others besides the American Medical Association. Newspapers have headlined the development of a doctor surplus, and the Department of Health, Education and Welfare under President Carter not only hoped that medical schools would reduce the size of their classes but argued (with the AMA) that physician oversupply would cause dramatically rising costs. In effect, they were arguing that the laws of supply and demand do not work in the medical profession. But there are growing indications that the increased supply of doctors is already having an effect. One example is a rapidly growing innovation known as the *preferred provider* program. Under this system, a group of doctors contracts with an insurance company, an employer, or a union and agrees to treat patients sent by the contractor for a fraction of their normal fees. In other words, doctors are cutting prices to get more patients. In a sponsored radio ad campaign in New York City, a corporation is offering home visits by physicians. In Westchester County, New York, a newspaper lists doctors willing to give senior citizens 10 percent to 25 percent fee reductions, to accept Medicare assignment fees as full payment, and to make house calls (*Wall Street Journal*, August 16, 1982). The laws of supply and demand still operate, even in the medical care profession.

SUMMARY

The growing costs of medical programs in this country stem from a mixture of past restrictions on supply, soaring demand as a consequence of zero or below-market prices for Medicare and Medicaid patients, third-party insurance, and the growing costs of malpractice suits; but it is still true that increasing the supply of doctors will help reduce those costs.

DISCUSSION QUESTIONS

1. The more opportunity individuals have to pass medical care costs on to third parties such as insurance companies, the less incentive they have to take care of themselves. The insurance industry calls this a problem of moral hazard. Is there any way this problem can be resolved to help reduce medical care costs?
2. Some have argued that doctors should be able to advertise just like any other group of persons offering services for sale. Do you agree or disagree? Why or why not?

11

the economics of
Advertising

Advertising is among the oldest of human activities. We can think of many "posters" from the ancient world. In its modern form, advertising began in England around 1850 together with the upsurge of the popular press. The wide availability of penny newspapers provided a ready audience for advertising that business could not overlook. The first major products to be advertised in these newspapers were proprietary, or patent, medicines and more respectable products such as cocoa, sewing machines, and tea. But it wasn't until advertising caught on in the United States that there was a rapid development of the technology. Kellogg originally promoted health foods as a proprietary remedy for alimentary tract problems. That company soon recognized that by advertising it could sell health foods as breakfast cereals. In 1913, the first truly modern national advertising campaign began with Camels, the first American blend of cigarettes, and cigarette makers have continued to be among the greatest innovators in advertising.

Every year businesses in the United States spend over $65 billion in advertising. To many, this tremendous sum represents a waste of society's resources. Lately, however, a number of researchers have started to show that while advertising does cost society resources, ultimately it can, under certain circumstances, lead to lower overall prices for consumers. How can that be? After all, a business has to make a profit and if advertising expenses are added on to production expenses, then the profit must end up at a higher price to the consumer. This logic is correct as far as it goes. What is missing is that crucial element called competition. As we shall see in this chapter, some industries' advertising causes prices to drop because it forces more competition on the businesses in that industry.

In the retail business, there is something called a markup, which is the percentage increase over the wholesale price that the retailer charges to the customer. This is also called the distribution margin. Consider the toy industry. According to one researcher, distribution margins were almost 50 percent in the 1950s. By the early 1970s, that margin had fallen to 33 percent. This was not caused by a change in heart by retailers—they didn't become less interested in profits. Rather, the toy industry started to advertise quite massively, especially on TV. Until the 1950s, the American toy industry had been essentially an unadvertised market. In 1955, however, the Mattel Company of California started advertising toy burp guns on the Mickey Mouse Club Show. Well before Christmas, Mattel burp guns were no longer on retail shelves. From then on, the toy industry was hooked on TV advertising.

At the same time, a revolutionary feature developed in retail marketing—the discount stores. In 1960, discount stores had total sales of $2 billion; 10 years later, they had sales of almost $30 billion. The discounters found something quite interesting: the turnover was very rapid on heavily advertised toys. Thus, the toys could be sold very profitably at far below the suggested retail price and the discounters would still make a profit.

At Christmas time, for example, a $5 toy that was advertised at $2.99 drew large crowds. At the beginning of the 1970s, discount stores accounted for 30 percent of retail toy sales and their toy departments were averaging a distribution markup of only 26 percent. Clearly, traditional retailers had to compete by cutting their prices also. In fact, branded, well-advertised items make comparison shopping easier and hence increase price competition among retailers.

Let's consider another industry which has been forbidden by law to advertise in some states: eyeglasses and eyeglass examinations. Many states have banned any advertising for these products or services. Such a ban affects the consumer directly in one important way. The consumer must expend more time and resources to find out about the various prices offered for the same product or service in his or her geographical area. In other words, the full price of eyeglasses will consist of the purchase price, the cost of time and transportation to obtain the eyeglasses, and the cost of obtaining the knowledge about where to find them. The more knowledge consumers have of alternative prices in an industry, the less will be the variation in prices from optician to optician.[1] One hypothesis would then be that advertising increases consumers' knowledge of alternative prices and thereby reduces the variation in prices in a given market area. Moreover, the only way that lower price–high volume sellers can exist is by informing great numbers of consumers from a rather large geographical area that eyeglasses are available at a lower price. If advertising is prohibited, such lower price–high volume sellers may not be able to exist.

A study on the effects of advertising on the price of eyeglasses was done by Professor Lee Benham. His data were for

[1] This comes from the modern argument for advertising that assumes imperfect information. Firms lower prices in order to increase sales. If customers find it extremely costly to discover differences in price among competing firms, each firm will tend to face a fairly inelastic demand schedule and charge a higher markup over marginal costs. Consequently, cartels find it easier to enforce the cartel price if the cost associated with price search can be increased. This is why they are in favor of laws prohibiting advertising.

1963, when approximately three-fourths of the states had some regulations against advertising. Benham presented two sets of results. First he compared all individuals in states with and without advertising restrictions and found that, on average, individuals in states with restrictions paid $6.70 more per pair of eyeglasses than those in states without restrictions. He also compared states having maximum and minimum restrictions during the year. Texas and the District of Columbia had virtually no restrictions, whereas North Carolina had extensive restrictions in force for a number of years. This comparison showed a mean difference in the price of eyeglasses that was even more dramatic—$19.50. Benham stated that though this was probably an overestimate, it did indicate that a difference existed. What we see is that in most states that allow advertising, larger firms or chains of firms advertise relatively more than others and thus keep prices down.

We can note here that the banning of advertising would tend to benefit the largest firms in an industry. After all, the largest firms have the most number of products outstanding. These products are in and of themselves advertisements for the firms. If, for example, the Federal Trade Commission banned all advertising for all types and makes of cars, General Motors would certainly benefit more than Honda. Can you imagine how much more difficult it would have been for Honda to introduce its cars in competition with General Motors' cars had it not been able to advertise on TV, in newspapers, and in magazines?

The banning of advertising has had dramatic effects in other industries too. In 1976, Congress banned the advertising of cigarettes on television in response to the Surgeon General's finding that cigarette smoking could lead to lung cancer. It was argued that captive TV watchers should not be subjected to the advertising of a hazardous product. The results of such a ban were just the opposite of the desired effect. The lack of cigarette advertising on TV has caused two distinct phenomena, both of which have led to possible increased health problems. Prior to the banning of cigarette advertising on TV, the American Cancer Society and the antismoking lobbyists succeeded in forcing free antismoking ads on TV. Under the Fairness Doctrine promulgated by the Federal Communications Commission, networks are supposed to air *both* sides of the story (as if there were only two sides to every argument). Thus, if TV networks were accepting money for cigarette advertisements, it was argued they must also accept antismoking ads (and for free). Thus, prior to 1976, there were several antismoking ads a day on each network. After the ban on TV advertising of cigarettes, however, the networks were no longer obligated under the Fairness Doctrine to show antismoking ads for free. Thus, the number of antismoking ads dropped dramatically. Apparently such ads were having an effect, especially among teenagers and women, for the percentage of teenagers and women who smoke has been rising since the time cigarette TV ads were banned. Perhaps that is a coincidence, but perhaps not.

The other phenomenon that may be leading to increased health hazards on the part of the American public results from the fact that TV advertising is a powerful, and perhaps the single most effective, means to introduce new cigarettes into the marketplace. Once people are set on smoking a particular brand of cigarette, it is hard to get them to change or to be aware of new brands; but TV advertising did just that—it made them aware of what was available. Professor Ben Klein has found that since the banning of advertising on TV, the introduction of new low tar, low nicotine cigarettes has dropped by 42 percent. Presumably, smokers benefit by switching to low tar, low nicotine cigarettes because they reduce the probability of lung disease in the future. Thus, the banning of such advertising has led consumers to stick with their old brands of cigarettes, which are likely to have higher levels of tar and nicotine and, hence, are more of a health hazard.

It is true that in a perfectly competitive world with perfectly homogeneous products, there would be no role for advertising.[2] But when we talk about advertising, are we referring to a world of monopolies? Not necessarily. Even a perfect competitor may

---

[2] This is because in a world of **marginal cost pricing**, there is no incentive to increase sales.

need to list its firm name in the Yellow Pages and put up a sign on the street to make people aware of its existence. When we go from there to the kind of advertising that we normally see, we are clearly not talking about perfect competitors but rather about firms that are selling differentiated products. Here we are entering the realm of either **monopolistic competition** or **oligopoly:** a realm where there are either a large number of sellers marketing slightly differentiated products, such as toothpaste or soap, or a small number of sellers, such as in automobiles. Advertising seems to be associated with such market structures, but it is not at all clear that advertising allows firms in those market structures to have more monopoly power. Indeed, it can be argued—and the evidence cited above supports the possibility—that advertising is necessary to allow for competition since it whittles away at the monopoly power of certain firms.

To be sure, heavily advertised brand names may appear to be associated with more, rather than less, monopoly power. After all, the firm that advertises the brand name successfully gets a large following of consumers who would rather "fight than switch." But the empirical evidence doesn't seem to support this suggestion. If we compare the market share of brand items in heavily advertised industries with the market share of brand items in little-advertised industries, we should, according to the above hypothesis, find that brand items have a constant share in the heavily advertised industries. In fact, it turns out that they have a less stable share in heavily advertised industries such as cosmetics and toiletries than in nonheavily advertised industries such as foods. Hence, a high level of advertising results in the high frequency of introduction of new products. This seems to be the case for cigarettes, cosmetics, and breakfast cereals. Advertising, then, may lead to a reduction in the amount of monopoly power due to brand names, rather than to an increase.

All of the above arguments should not be construed to mean that advertising is free of problems. Certainly fraudulent advertising has been, remains, and will continue to be a dilemma. Competitive market theory predicts that advertisers who engage in fraudulent representation will eventually be forced out of business. But how long will it take? Are there safeguards that can be put on advertising to prevent a socially excessive amount of misrepresentation? This is an important question that has yet to be answered by policymakers.

Another area of concern involves children's advertising. The Federal Trade Commission is seeking to ban certain forms of TV advertising aimed directly at the children's market, particularly on Saturday and Sunday morning cartoon shows, which raises the question of **consumer sovereignty.** Are we to consider five-year-olds as sovereign consumers capable of making correct choices? Or, alternatively, are we to consider their parents as sovereign consumers capable of guiding children's consumption decisions in an optimal manner? Certain members of the Federal Trade Commission answer these two questions "no" and therefore wish to put greater restrictions on children's ads, particularly on TV.

SUMMARY

Advertising appears to increase information about qualities and prices. In several studies, it has been shown that in states where certain products, such as eyeglasses, cannot be advertised, price variation is greater than in states where advertising for those products is allowed. When advertising is banned, such a ban benefits the largest firms in the industry because their products are advertisements in themselves. Also, potential competitors would have a very difficult time entering an industry in which advertising was banned. Extensive advertising typically occurs in less-than-competitive market structures. Nonetheless, it has not yet been proved that advertising creates monopoly power. Even in a world of less-than-perfect competition, fraudulent advertising should only be a temporary phenomenon.

DISCUSSION QUESTIONS

1. What about advertising that has no information content, such as "Buy the Uncola" or "Things go better with Coke." Does this type of advertising yield any benefit to the consumer?
2. Who pays for the cost of advertising?

12

the economics of
International Cartels

Every week 300 of the world's richest and most prestigious diamond dealers are invited to view the "sights" in an office on Fleet Street in London. These sights are uncut diamonds being sold by the Central Selling Organization, or CSO. The CSO's nine-story office building in London is popularly known as "the syndicate." Through it every year passes 80 percent of the supply of rough-cut diamonds in the world. One organization controls that 80 percent of the supply—DeBeers, the famous diamond company. In 1978, it marketed $2.5 billion worth of gems, a 23 percent increase over 1977. DeBeers also produces about 35 percent of the world's diamonds. It's clearly in a good monopoly position. The 300 diamond dealers who come in every week are shown the diamonds and told the price. Haggling is essentially not allowed; in fact, it is rumored that if one haggles, one is not asked back.

If DeBeers were simply the producer of 35 percent of the

world's diamonds, it might not have such an effective control on the market price of diamonds; but it has been successful in forming a very strong cartel-type arrangement in which it is the sole marketing agent of another 45 percent of the world's rough-cut diamonds. In this way it becomes an effective monopoly: it controls the sales, or more specifically, the amount of sales that are offered to diamond dealers throughout the world. It can effectively police the number of diamonds offered for sale every year. It can do what a monopolist wishes to do—restrict output and thereby raise the price above what it would be in a perfectly competitive situation.

Another successful international cartel, and one to which we alluded elsewhere in this book, is OPEC, the Organization of Petroleum Exporting Countries. In 1960, OPEC started as an organization designed to assist the oil-exporting countries. By 1970, it included Abu Dhabi, Algeria, Indonesia, Iran, Iraq, Kuwait, Libya, Nigeria, Qatar, Saudi Arabia, and Venezuela; later a few other countries, including Ecuador, joined the group. During the 1960s, OPEC's success was limited because an ever-expanding supply of oil kept just ahead of demand. As demand grew, new discoveries expanded the supplies so fast that nominal well-head prices for crude oil actually fell slightly between 1960 and 1970. Then in 1970 and 1971, the rate of growth of the demand for crude oil tapered off. Also in 1970, Libya, which had become a major supplier of crude oil to Western European markets, had a revolution. The new regime cut output sharply in a partly political move against the oil companies to which concessions had been granted by the previous regime. Libya's cutback made sizable price increases possible in 1971. These increases were ratified by the other members of OPEC in agreements drawn up in Tripoli and Teheran. Much of the success of this rise in prices was credited to OPEC, although some observers contend that Libya was alone responsible and had no help from OPEC.

However the main ingredient in OPEC's success was the outbreak of war in the Middle East in 1973. In the wake of this war, Saudi Arabia, Kuwait, and a few smaller Arab countries agreed to greatly cut back their production of crude oil, thus paving the way for large price increases. Remember that the only way to raise prices when one is a pure monopolist is to cut back on production and sales. Thus, OPEC members could have an effective cartel arrangement only if some or all of them cut back on production and sales. Since Saudi Arabia, which accounts for the bulk of the oil production in the Middle East, did cut back greatly in 1973, the cartel arrangement worked, and continued to work for several years. The total profits for the oil-exporting countries were increased greatly as a result.

The effect of OPEC cartelization activities on world oil prices was dramatic. On January 1, 1973, one could buy Saudi Arabian crude oil at $2.12 a barrel. Within one year, the price of crude had risen to $7.61 per barrel; by 1975, to $10.50; and by 1978, to $14.57.

Other international cartels have been formed, many of them involved with internationally traded commodities. The International Bauxite Association (IBA) has attempted to control the price of bauxite around the world. The International Tin Agreement has existed since before World War II. The Organization of Banana-Exporting Countries has tried to duplicate OPEC's success. There are producer cartels in iron ore, mercury, tea, tropical timber, natural rubber, nickel, cobalt, tungsten, columbium, pepper, tantalum, and quinine, and probably many more. Not all of them are successful. We now ask the question: What are the necessary ingredients to a successful cartel arrangement?

A cartel must meet four basic requirements if it is to be successful.

1. It must control a large share of total actual output and potential. It must not face substantial competition from outsiders.
2. Available substitutes must be limited. In other words, the price elasticity of demand for the product in question must be fairly low; that is, there must be relatively (but not completely) **inelastic demand.**
3. The demand for the cartel's product must be relatively

stable, regardless of business conditions. If this is not the case, then the amount sold at any given price will be greater during economic **expansions** than during **recessions,** and the cartel will find it difficult to maintain any given price and output combination for very long.

4. Producers must be willing and able to withhold sufficient amounts of their product to affect the market. Each member must resist the temptation to cheat. And consumers must not be able to have large stockpiles of the product on which to draw.

There are probably other conditions that would make a cartel's success probability even greater, but these can be considered the basic ones.

A big cause of cartel instability is cheating. When there are many firms or countries in a cartel arrangement, there will always be some that are unhappy with the situation. They will want to cheat by charging a slightly lower price than the one stipulated by the cartel. Members who are producing a small percentage of the total output of the cartel essentially face a very elastic demand curve if they cheat and no one else does. A small drop in price by a cheater will result in a very large increase in total revenues.

There will always be cartel members who figure that it will pay them to cut prices. Each firm will try to do this, thinking that the others will not do the same thing. Or a firm may decide that other firms are going to cheat anyway, so why shouldn't it be the first? Obviously, though, when a sufficient number of firms in the cartel try to cheat, the cartel breaks up. We would expect, therefore, that as long as the cartel is not maintained by legislation, there will be a constant threat to its existence. Its members will have a large incentive to cut prices, and once a couple of members do that, the rest may follow.

Consider, for example, the failure of the copper cartel, CIPEC, the Intergovernmental Council of Copper Exporting Countries. CIPEC was founded in 1967 by Chile, Zambia, Zaire, and Peru. It still exists, but it has never managed to show any muscle in world markets. In 1974 the price of copper started falling. From April to the end of December, it had dropped by 55 percent. CIPEC was powerless to bring it back up. Why? Because most of the developing countries are unwilling or unable to limit their output of copper. There isn't a Saudi Arabia of the copper world that is willing to cut back 50 percent on production so that the rest of the cartel can enjoy higher prices. Remember, the only way to keep prices up is to keep production down.

The coffee cartel hasn't fared much better. The price of coffee has gone up and down like a yoyo. Every time the price starts falling, big coffee producers such as Colombia and Brazil urge other producing nations to cut back. They do so at the annual meeting of the Council of International Coffee Organization (ICO). Moreover, ICO has found out what the price elasticity of demand for coffee really is. Each time the price has jumped, the quantity demanded has fallen, sometimes dramatically. In 1977, for example, the general manager of Colombia's coffee growers' federation thought that the 60 cents increase per pound on the average in retail prices during the last two years had caused consumption to drop by 15 percent. His suggestion to other coffee producers at that time? Lower prices. In other words, even a strong cartel cannot face up to the possibility of consumers cutting back on the consumption of a higher-priced good.

Cartel instability, or lack of success, is not confined to business firms or even to nations engaging in international commodities selling. Have you ever noticed how short-lived a homemakers' boycott of a supermarket is? There are so many members in that particular cartel that it is difficult for one of them not to "cheat" and actually go out and buy some food from the supermarket. It is impossible to police the large number of homemakers involved.

Consider one more example, which is hypothetical. If you are in a class of 100 students whose exams will be graded on a curve, how easily could all of you get together and agree to cut down study time? Would your cartel be successful? The answer, of course, depends on each individual student's incentive to cheat. If only one student were to cheat and study longer than all the others, that student would get a higher grade than he or she would otherwise have received. If enough students do this, the cartel will break down.

Several of the cartels discussed in this chapter are under serious pressure at the writing of this edition. DeBeers diamond cartel has been singularly unsuccessful in keeping the price of diamonds from falling. Starting in 1980, the demand for all collectibles and so-called real, or hard, assets fell dramatically as individuals, particularly in the United States, no longer sought inflation hedges. Moreover, there was a worldwide recession starting in 1981. In spite of a reduction in the quantity of diamonds supplied to the market, the wholesale price of diamonds fell by over 60 percent from their historical highs at the end of the 1970s. Also, a big diamond find occurred in Australia. Perhaps DeBeers will be successful in also controlling the output of that diamond supply, but if it is not, the cartel may collapse. The OPEC cartel was also singularly unsuccessful in keeping the price of crude oil at historically high levels. The price of crude oil fell in the beginning of the 1980s in nominal terms, which means that it fell even more in real (or inflation-corrected) terms. The many years of relatively high crude oil prices finally had their effect — the worldwide supply increased dramatically over a 10-year period from the first "energy crisis."

SUMMARY

Cartel arrangements are methods by which cartel members restrict supply in order to keep prices high. After all, the law of demand states that price and quantity demanded are inversely related. There is no way to sell the same quantity at a higher price, other things held constant. Therefore, potential cartel founders must realize that they must be successful in restricting output in order to raise prices. Several cartels have done just that, among them the diamond cartel and the oil cartel. In all cartel arrangements, there is an incentive for cartel members to cheat. Provided that they can cheat without being detected, they will make a higher profit. When all cartel members simultaneously attempt to cheat and are effective in so doing, the cartel breaks down and prices fall.

DISCUSSION QUESTIONS

1. Why are all cartels inherently unstable?
2. Would it be easier to form a cartel in a market with many producers or one with very few producers?

13

the economics of
The
Stock Market

Many people dream of becoming rich. Some will become rich in later years when they inherit wealth, that is, **stocks**—**common stock** or **preferred stock**, **bonds**, real estate, valuable paintings, and other kinds of property that their parents or relatives own. Most people, however, will not be so fortunate. To attain wealth, those individuals will have to work hard and put their **savings** into wise **investments.**

A distinction must be made here between putting savings into investments that will pay a steady rate of return year after year, and investing them in schemes to make a "killing" over the course of a few months or a year. Some individuals choose the latter course in an attempt to "get rich quick." Most people, however, do not gamble with their accumulated savings. Rather, they invest their savings in one or more of the following areas: savings accounts, long-term bonds, pension plans, and the stock market.

Furthermore, they usually leave most of their savings in the investment for 20–40 years before withdrawing it for retirement expenses.

There are, of course, many get-rich-quick schemes involving the stock market. One of the most popular is picking the "right" stocks to buy at the "right" time. But what are the right stocks and when is the right time? Obviously, they are stocks whose purchase price is currently low but whose selling price will be extremely high in time.

Perhaps your parents or friends deal in the stock market —that is, they buy and sell stock. If so, you have probably heard some strange words about "the market" in their conversations. They may talk about "hot" tips, or reasons why the market might rise or fall, or about a broker's forecasts of stock prices.

When one wants information about an illness, for example, one generally consults a doctor, or even goes to a specialist. If one wants information about how to repair a car, one may go to another type of specialist—an automobile mechanic. Thus, when seeking information about the stock market, logic would seem to suggest that one should go to a stock specialist—a broker.

This reasoning is partly accurate. A stockbroker can provide information about how the stock market operates and about the costs of buying and selling stocks. The broker can also lead the investor away from very risky stocks—those giving the investor a small chance of making large gains but a large chance of losing everything. The broker can give advice concerning the right combination of stocks and bonds and can suggest different types of stocks for the investor's particular needs in terms of security and income in the future. But the broker is generally *not* the person who can make the investor rich quick. The broker *cannot* tell the investor, with absolute certainty, the best way to invest his or her dollars in the market.

Look in the Yellow Pages of the telephone book under "Stock and Bond Brokers" and pick a name at random. If you were to call one of the brokerage firms listed, you could ask to speak with a broker. (A broker is a salesperson, but he or she may have the title of "account executive.") The following example illustrates what would probably happen.

When you got the broker on the phone, you would tell him or her that you have $5000 to invest, and ask for advice. Before the broker tells you anything, he or she will ask you what your goals are. Do you want steady income from your investment of $5000? Do you want growth stocks that will provide a reasonable **capital gain** in the future?

After you tell the broker the strategy you want to take, he or she will probably advise you on the best stocks to buy and then predict (guess) whether the stock market will go up or down in the next few months. The broker's opinion will sound very informed and authoritative.

Strange as it may seem, though, the broker's advice on how to invest your money generally is not any better than anyone else's advice. In fact, *the chances of the broker's being right are no greater than the chances of your being right!* Does this sound improbable? Perhaps. Yet the fact remains that economists, statisticians, and investors have examined and tested this proposition from numerous angles. And all have reached the same conclusion.

You have probably never studied investing before. How can you guess about what the stock market will do? Or about how profitable a company may be in the future?

The stock market is one of the most competitive markets in the world. Competition among investors means that all investors try to do as well as they can. In doing so, each investor must compete with all other investors. Investors' efforts to gain higher profits are what make the stock market highly competitive. It is more competitive than most other markets because literally millions of investors trade in it. In addition, it is even more competitive because of the availability of information about it at relatively low cost.

Almost any daily newspaper will give you information about the price of stocks on the New York and the American exchanges as well as on certain regional stock exchanges. Stock price quotations are published daily in the financial section of the newspaper. In addition, current stock price information is available from most brokerage firms. These firms have tickertape-type electronic machines that receive price changes for various stocks almost as fast as they are announced, even though the firm may be more than 3000 miles from the stock exchange.

Information about a specific company also rapidly becomes widely known. As soon as a company announces its profits, literally millions of people learn about it. Such information is not as readily available as the prices of listed stocks, but it flows quite freely within the American economy.

The point is that by the time one investor reads about what a company, an industry, or, for that matter, the national economy is going to do, most other investors have also read it. The information is **public information**—available to anyone and everyone at very low cost. Public information cannot help you in your plan to get rich quick.

To understand why public information will not help, let us look at an example. Suppose a company in your neighborhood has discovered a substitute for gasoline. You read about the discovery in the newspaper. After reading the article, you decide the company's stock would be an excellent purchase because the company should make a great deal of money from its discovery.

But think about the idea more carefully. Will not everyone else think the same way? In fact, will not many people who learned about the discovery *before* you also realize that the company stands to make higher profits? Certainly they will. Some will already have bought stock in the company. As they bid against each other to buy stock, the price of the stock will start to rise. By the time you read about the discovery, competing investors will have *already* bid up the price of the stock to reflect the "new" information. Hence, by the time vital information becomes public, it is essentially useless to someone trying to get rich quick.

Because the stock market is so highly competitive and because information about it flows so freely, it follows a **random walk**. The market as a whole has trends, such as the general upward trend from its beginning that reflects, among other things, the reinvestment of company earnings. However, the prices of specific stocks and the average of all stock prices exhibit a random walk relative to the overall market trend. Any examination of past stock prices will not yield useful information for predicting future prices. Years of academic research have left little doubt that the stock market follows a random walk. If a person were to find out otherwise, he or she could get rich quickly.

Some individuals are superior forecasters of what will happen in the economy. They may have some special innate ability, or they may have developed a forecasting method that is superior to anyone else's. As long as the methods used by these individuals do not become common knowledge, these individuals can indeed make higher-than-normal profits in the stock market. It is the ability to *interpret* public information (and **inside information**, also) that gives some individuals the edge in the stock market.

SUMMARY

The market for publicly traded shares of stock is one of the most highly competitive in the world. Information about the future profitability of companies is quickly dispersed throughout the buying public. Therefore, that knowledge rarely, if ever, allows an individual to make a higher-than-normal rate of return in the stock market. The prices of stocks follow a random walk, and you cannot predict the future of the price of stocks by using past information. Only individuals with superior talents at interpreting public information have a chance to make a higher-than-normal rate of return, on average, in the stock market.

DISCUSSION QUESTIONS

1. The stock market is highly competitive. Therefore, what average rate of return can you predict you will make by "wheeling and dealing" in the stock market?
2. Rates of return in the stock market during the 1970s were historically very low. Using the competitive model, what can you predict will happen to the amount of resources flowing into publicly owned companies listed on stock exchanges?

14

the economics of
Cents-off Coupons

The producers of food and other products sold in the hundreds of thousands of retail food outlets across the United States sometimes use "cents-off" coupons to attract customers. If these producers are competitive, why do they do so, since this practice is not consistent with a model of pure competition? Because the practice *is* consistent with a model of monopolistic competition, which allows for slight degrees of monopoly power by individual producers. We will show that the use of cents-off coupons is a form of price discrimination.

The full price of a product includes not only the monetary price but also the implicit opportunity cost of the time spent searching out the product and purchasing it (and the time needed to consume it). We can assume that, all else being equal, the higher one values time saved from shopping, the less time one will spend in seeking out lower-cost shopping arrangements. In other words, a person who places a higher value on time, relative to money, will spend more money to save shopping time. This means that a person who places a high value on time will exhibit a less elastic demand curve in a given store than a person who places a lower value on time.

Let us assume that there is a strong correlation between a person's wealth and the value he or she puts on time, that is, that richer people, on average, value their time more highly than do poorer people. It follows that a richer person's relative price elasticity of demand will be less than a poorer person's. Now the suppliers of the various products sold in retail food outlets are confronted with two classes of consumers: those with relatively less elastic demand and those with relatively more elastic demand. The supplier's problem is to separate these two classes and charge the richer customer a higher price than the poorer customer. One way that this can be (and is) done is to offer a rebate only to those customers who are willing to incur a time cost to obtain that rebate. The rebate is in the form of cents-off coupons, which are available only to those customers who take time to cut them out of magazines, keep track of them if they are received in the mail, or obtain them by some other means. These cents-off coupons must be kept with the person, taken to the retail food outlet, and then exchanged at the cash register for a reduction in the price charged for the particular item. All of these activities require time. Thus, poorer people, whom we are assuming can be used as proxies for the relatively more elastic demanders, pay a lower money price for their purchases in retail food outlets when they utilize cents-off coupons. The richer customers, with relatively less elastic demand, refuse to be bothered by cents-off coupons because of the time cost involved, and as a result get no discount at all.

If the above cents-off coupon model is useful, it presents us with some testable implications.

1. We can predict that cents-off coupons will be offered relatively less often in cases where the price of a single purchase is large. This is because the receiver of a valuable coupon for a large purchase would incur a small

time cost relative to the value of the coupon. In other words, not enough differential time costs would be imposed to discourage relatively low elasticity demanders from collecting the cents-off coupons. This implication is consistent with the fact that cents-off coupons are almost exclusively used for relatively low-priced items sold in retail food stores.

2. We can predict that when the commodity is a personal service, relatively few cents-off coupons will be used. The cents-off coupon is a substitute for price discounting, and the differentiation in quality of services offered already accomplishes the price-discriminating goal. This implication is consistent with the observation that beauty parlors and barber shops typically do not give cents-off coupons.

SUMMARY

Even in the competitive world of retail food, each retailer has a slight amount of market power. In other words, monopolistic competition prevails. In order to exploit their slight market power, individual sellers offer cents-off coupons. This allows them to price discriminate, effectively offering lower prices to individuals who place a lower value on their time and higher prices to individuals who place a higher value on their time. In general, the former are poorer customers and the latter are richer customers.

DISCUSSION QUESTIONS

1. Why is monopolistic competition the appropriate model for food producers? Does it seem to be the appropriate model for other industries? Why or why not?
2. How does the use of cents-off coupons allow the monopolistic competitor to price discriminate among customers with different price elasticities of demand?

part three
Factor Markets

INTRODUCTION

Supply and demand analysis applies to the market for factors of production. These factors of production may be in the form of **labor** or **capital.** Most of the chapters in this part deal with the factor we call labor. In Chapter 15, we analyze the draft as a system in which labor is obtained at a below-market wage by using the police power of the state. In Chapter 19, which deals with **minimum wages,** we find out what happens when the purchaser of labor is not allowed to pay a wage rate below some government-mandated minimum. Basically, the result is similar to what happens with agricultural price-support systems—surpluses occur. In this case, we call the surplus unemployment.

In Chapter 16, whose subject is professional sports, we analyze labor market restrictions in which the purchasers of the labor input band together to form a monopoly. This type of monopoly is called a **monopsony**—single buyer. An effective monopsony can reduce the wage rate obtained by the individuals affected, and that is indeed what has occurred off and on in professional sports. In Chapter 20, we analyze the use of labor and capital by the police as if police personnel were attempting to minimize their costs for any given output. The output is crime prevention and the inputs are labor and capital.

Again, we caution the reader that we are not analyzing individuals' thought processes, but rather their observed behavior patterns and the way those behavior patterns change according to the changing constraints.

15

the economics of
The Draft

When the war in Vietnam ended, soon thereafter so did the draft, which was replaced by an all-volunteer army. Not many years later, headlines about the "failure of the volunteer armed forces" proliferated. Senators and members of Congress alike cried out for a revival of the draft. Before we can understand what is at issue, we have to take a look at the beginnings of the military conscription system that was with us for almost two centuries, first instituted during the war for independence. Massachusetts and Virginia used conscription in 1777. On February 6, 1778, Congress recommended that the other colonies follow suit, but because France sent troops, it was unnecessary to initiate a general draft. During the War of 1812, apparently Connecticut and Massachusetts threatened to secede from the Union over the draft issue. But when the draft almost became law in 1814, those two state legislatures were ready to guarantee the protection of their men from the federal government draft.

In April 1862, the Confederacy started universal conscription. By 1863, the North saw fit to pass the Enrollment Bill. Its passage led to bloodshed and violence. Indeed, in 1863 police and militia battled antidraft mobs in the streets of New York for three days.[1] But although there was a draft during the Civil War, men who were conscripted were allowed to "buy" someone else to go in their stead. Therefore, even though the method of conscription was arbitrary, the final determination of who would go to war was more flexible. For example, a lawyer who found himself conscripted had the option of paying someone else to replace him. As long as the price he paid was lower than the amount he could earn by remaining at work, he would benefit financially from the arrangement. Since many workers did not earn as much as a lawyer could (that is, their opportunity costs were lower), it was not hard to find a replacement—who would also benefit —at a mutually agreeable price. Understandably, relatively few of the fighting men in the Civil War came from higher-paying civilian occupations. Since a man's contribution to the economy can be roughly indicated by his salary, it can be said in economists' terminology that an *efficient*[2] *allocation of resources* resulted, since men worked (or fought) where their services were of most value.

Let's digress for a moment into a fuller discussion of this question of allocation of resources. Inefficiency exists whenever labor and machines are being used in such a manner that their full potential contribution to the output of the economy is not being realized. A change from an inefficient to an efficient allocation therefore results, by definition, in an increase in output. This does not mean that everyone will be better off. All changes in our economy carry certain costs, and those who incur these costs are worse off. But in theory, the increase in output allows those who bear the costs of the change to be fully compensated, assuming,

[1] Somewhat ironically, at that same time only about two percent of the Union army were draftees.
[2] The term "efficient" as used in economics does not have any connotation of "good," "desirable," or "best," but merely refers to the most productive use of available resources.

of course, that some institutional mechanism exists through which the compensating "side payment" can be carried out.

Now we return to the historical question of America's army-building techniques. During World War I, the form of conscription became a pure lottery, and draftees were not allowed to hire replacements. From the Civil War through the Korean War, a total of 14,448,330 men were inducted. Essentially the same economic analysis applies to all the men in those conflicts. Let's consider some economic aspects of the draft.

Costs that often go unnoticed are associated with any method of involuntary conscription. To simplify, let us analyze the military as though it were a business, referring to "managers" who hire and fire "workers" and who allocate part of their fixed yearly budget to pay for machines instead of men. When the Army obtains soldiers at a wage rate lower than that which would induce these men to join of their own free will, the military managers are obtaining incorrect information about the true costs of their operation. When labor is artificially underpriced (because of the draft), military management ends up using fewer machines and more men than they would otherwise have used. Why? The decision is made along the following lines: At a given price for men, the Army must consider the possibility of adding machinery either to aid the men or to replace them in certain jobs. If an additional adding machine will allow one man to do the work that two men would have done without the machine, management must look at the relative prices in order to decide rationally if the machine should be rented (or bought). If one man costs $100 a week and one adding machine rents for $25, the machine will be used. But if the price for the man falls to $20 a week, it is not economically worthwhile to rent a machine for the purpose of saving labor costs. Because draftees are, in fact, paid far below their "going price" on the labor market, or the price that would induce them to volunteer, we know that the military is using "too many" men. We may say, then, that conscription results in a higher-than-optimal men/machine ratio in the military. As we will see later, this inevitably costs society more resources than are necessary for any desired level of national defense.

Another added cost resulted from the fact that conscription was typically for a period of only two years. In all likelihood, in a military composed entirely of volunteers obtained in the same way that firms hire their workers (i.e., paid adequate wages), the turnover time would be longer than two years. In fact, since the Army must certainly pay much higher wages than those offered under a draft system, its management is making a relatively greater effort to ensure that turnover time is substantially longer.

Turnover involves very real costs. When a soldier comes into the service, he is "green" and must be trained. Training involves the use of resources such as machines and other men's time. When a draftee's two years are up, someone else must be trained to fill his spot, at more cost.

In addition to the relatively high turnover costs associated with the draft, conscription also results in an inefficient allocation of men's talents once they are in the Army. In the civilian world one rarely sees college-trained men washing dishes and cleaning outhouses. Employers benefit from placing men where their training adds to productivity—that is, where they contribute most to the output of the firm. Not so in a draft army.

All draftees are obtained at the same price, whether they are Ph.D.s or functional illiterates. As in business, incentive probably exists for military management to use draftees most effectively, but the signals are not as apparent as in the civilian world where the highly differentiated salaries of workers of different quality are unmistakable. To hire a Ph.D., a business firm must pay more than it pays for an unschooled worker. Therefore it behooves the firm to get the most for its money by putting the Ph.D. to work at a task where he or she is most productive.

In addition to the above costs, the economy suffers an opportunity cost for every man drafted that is *totally independent of what draftees are paid.* The true cost to society of a draftee is what he could be earning as a civilian. When a man is paid $10,000 by an employer, we can usually assume that the employer is obtaining at least that amount in services; otherwise the arrangement would be terminated. If the same man is drafted, the economy is giving up about $10,000 worth of civilian productive services a year to obtain a much smaller amount in military services. *That* amount, and not the $1500 in Army pay he will receive, is the true annual cost of his induction.

Since a draft army pays (via tax dollars) only a small fraction of the true opportunity cost of draftees, who, then, pays the rest? Obviously, the draftees themselves bear the burden of an implicit tax that roughly equals the difference between their civilian pay and their Army pay.[3] But all suffer somewhat, because the output of nonmilitary goods and services is lower and more expensive since these men are not working at their civilian jobs (unless, of course, all draftees are taken from the ranks of the unemployed).[4]

This hidden tax aspect of the draft is certainly not new. Benjamin Franklin commented on it over 200 years ago in reviewing the court's opinion concerning the legality of impressment of American merchant seamen. He wrote:

> But if, as I suppose is often the case, the sailor who is pressed and obliged to serve for the defense of this trade at the rate of 25 shillings a month could have 3 pounds 15 shillings in the merchant service, you take from him 50 shillings a month; and if you have 100,000 in your service, you rob the honest part of society and their poor families of 250,000 pounds per month or three millions a year, and at the same time oblige them to hazard their lives in fighting for the defence of your trade.

Examination of the distribution of this implicit tax discloses that the draft system we used to have was highly favorable to the rich and highly unfavorable to the poor, mainly because of all the exemptions that were available to higher-income draft candidates. It was actually a highly **regressive tax**, in that the higher the income level, the lower the tax paid, on the average, mea-

---

[3] To the Army pay should be added the benefits of training and education obtained while in the service, plus any consumption value received ("Join the Army and see the world").

[4] Some say we benefit because military service "makes men out of boys," good citizens out of bad, and community leaders out of juvenile delinquents. Of course, there may be cheaper ways of obtaining these "goods."

sured as a percentage of income. Exemptions for those attending college and graduate school, which preceded the lottery system, merely amplified the regressive effects. What proportion of the poor and of minority races continues education past high school? Even under the lottery system, the rich had resources to call on: lawyers, doctors, and psychiatrists could help them avoid the draft. In 1969, of 283,000 men drafted, only 28,500 were college men. This figure represents 10 percent of the total drafted, whereas in the total male college-age population of the United States, 40 percent are in college. The end of college deferments has therefore lessened, but has not cured, the regressive effect of the "draft tax."[5]

The American public is told that the all-volunteer army is too expensive. This complaint is totally beside the point. Society pays for the army whether or not the nation's youths are drafted. Nor is it true that not enough volunteers have been found. Because the final three months of 1978 showed enlistments at only 90 percent of desired enlistments, this does not mean our military strength has decreased. At the end of 1978, the army had 2000 soldiers more than it had budgeted for. The shortage in recruits was more than made up by an excess of reenlistments. Only in specialized areas, such as medicine and the reserves, has there been any problem. Those shortfalls can be eliminated any time that Congress decides to pay the price to attract a desired number and quality of reservists and medical personnel.[6]

When we examine the data on quality, it is not at all clear what Congress means when it says that the all-volunteer army has failed. When we had the draft in 1964, 68 percent of recruits

---

[5] Note that the lottery may be even less efficient than the draft with exemptions, because with the draft those men whose contributions to civilian output are high do not get drafted. This does not, of course, mean that exemptions are "good."

[6] One of the reasons there is such a demand for medical personnel is because the services insist that uniformed personnel provide medical services to both enlisted personnel and their families wherever they are stationed. Presumably, the military could simply provide medical insurance as a fringe benefit rather than provide medical services directly.

were high school graduates. In 1979, that number rose to almost 70 percent. In 1964, 1 of 7 recruits was classified in the lowest mental group eligible for recruitment. By 1979, the ratio had dropped to 1 in 20.

As in all economic situations, an insufficient supply can be blamed on too low a price. The fact is that the military is not paid competitive wage rates. In 1972, military wage rates were indeed competitive. By 1980, however, they had fallen significantly. It is therefore not surprising that the military had such a hard time filling its manpower quotas. The Reagan Administration did, however, make some attempt to raise military pay scales to a more competitive rate.

One way for the military to reduce its labor costs would be to recruit already-trained civilian personnel for middle-level positions. Individuals between the ages of 30 and 50 could be hired to perform technical and management jobs for the military while remaining civilians. Today, the military basically draws all of its middle- and upper-level personnel from within the ranks. Thus, it is forced to keep and train soldiers to fill important technical and management positions. Why can't it go out into the labor market and hire civilians, who would remain civilians, to perform technical and management jobs? The holders of such jobs do not operate "on the front." Do they really need to be soldiers?

SUMMARY

Conscription is, in effect, a type of **exploitation** of military personnel. Rather than pay a market-clearing wage rate, the government chooses, under a system of draft, to pay a below-market-clearing wage rate and to require certain individuals to "serve their country." From society's point of view, the cost of the army is the same whether military personnel are paid nothing, one-half their market wage rate, or their full market wage rate. The cost of the military is the full social opportunity cost — the equivalent of what each individual could be earning as a civilian. The social opportunity cost of the army does not depend on who pays for the military. A draft system effectively taxes those who are drafted. An all-volunteer army is neither cheaper nor more expensive than a conscription army.

DISCUSSION QUESTIONS

1. How is it possible to have a "shortage" of military personnel?
2. If we were to go back to a full system of the draft, who would benefit and who would lose?

16

the economics of
Professional Sports

In 1981 the baseball season was short—very short, in fact. Why? Because there was a strike. For 50 days of that season, players and team owners could not reach an agreement. Apparently, the major bone of contention was the so-called free agent issue. What was that all about? Well, it involved the freedom of players to seek, without restrictions, better employment opportunities within the baseball industry at the end of a specified contractual period with their current team. Until 1981, there were serious restrictions on the movement of baseball players among teams. These restrictions were based on the "reserve clause" in a player's contract, which gave the team exclusive rights to the player's services until he was sold, traded, or released by the team. As a result of this clause many players brought antitrust suits against professional baseball league owners. For example, baseball player Curt Flood brought such a suit in the 1970s. When the case reached the Supreme Court in 1972, Flood lost, even though Justice Harry A. Blackmun admitted that the reserve clause was "an aberration."

As a result of the strike, the baseball players were relatively successful in eliminating the pernicious effects of the reserve clause. Football players, who went on strike in the fall of 1982, were not, however, as successful as the baseball players. Currently they are working under a system that binds a player exclusively to the team which holds his contract. Modifications have been made, but the reserve clause still seems relatively effective. To understand why the reserve clause has been used in baseball, basketball, and football for so many years, we will first look at a labor market which has no reserve clause—the labor market for gardeners. Most gardeners charge what they think is the "going" price for their services. If one charges considerably less than this price, some potential additional customers will eventually find out. He will then find himself with many new requests for his services. If he is not willing to put extra hours into gardening, he will have to decide on one, or a combination, of the following courses: (1) lower the quality of his service so that each job requires less time, and thus squeeze in more customers; (2) refuse the additional work; or (3) raise his prices so that certain customers, present or potential, will not be interested in obtaining his services. Obviously, the first choice is equivalent to the third, since a change in quality at the same price exerts the same economic effect as a change in price for the same quality.

On the other hand, a gardener who does not have enough work and wishes to attract more customers is free to lower his price or raise the quality of his services. That is, gardeners can compete among themselves to maximize their own individual incomes. To be sure, not all gardeners do this.

Now let's assume that a particular gardener gains a reputation for doing exceptionally good work. If he already has a full schedule, a potential customer will have to offer some incentive to gain his services on a regular basis. An adequate incentive might persuade the gardener to do one of the following: (1) work more intensively, (2) work longer hours and take fewer holidays, or (3) drop one of his former customers.

The usual form of incentive is an offer of higher wages, although incentives are not always monetary. In any case, by employing such tactics, people desiring to obtain gardeners' services are competing among themselves. Although not all homeowners take the trouble to find out which gardener in the neighborhood gives the best service at the lowest price, some do.

We have just described the workings of a competitive market in gardening. Gardeners are free to vary the price, quantity, and quality of the service they sell. Homeowners are free to vary the price (wage) they offer, and the quantity and quality of service they demand. Theoretically, gardeners end up getting a wage that just equals the value of their services (i.e., they are paid the value of their marginal product). Buyers of gardeners' services end up paying for the opportunity cost of these services, no more, no less (i.e., they must pay the value of the gardeners' marginal product).

What would happen if all homeowners in the country got together and decided to institute a "gardening reserve clause"? The clause would require that each individual gardener work for only one homeowner (or, more realistically in this case, for one group of owners). The gardener could not work anywhere else unless the owner of the contract with the reserve clause decided that he, the owner, wanted to sell or trade the contract. Notice that one crucial aspect of the previously described competitive market has been eliminated: gardeners cannot seek out the most advantageous job opportunities or compete for business, because only the homeowners can initiate a move. It is surely apparent that such restraint would prevent gardeners from seeking employment that would maximize their income and that it could leave them worse off than they were under free and competitive conditions.

They not only could, but most certainly *would*, be worse off if all homeowners then got together to form a cartel with the express agreement that they would not compete among themselves for gardeners' contracts. Competition in the gardening market would be stifled on both sides: among the sellers of gardening services and among the buyers of those services.[1]

What is pure hypothesis in our example was reality in the world of baseball for many years. The major league teams had made agreements among themselves which yielded a very special players' contract. Since the term included an agreement not to tamper with a player "reserved" by any team, the contracting club, in effect, held a unilateral option on the player's services for the following year. Once the player signed, he accepted all agreements made between teams; therefore, his only course was to attempt to get the highest possible salary from his particular team, with no help from competing teams. The player's choice was simple: to accept the offered salary or not to play baseball—at least not with any U.S. major league team.

The reserve clause allowed a baseball team to restrain the workings of the job market for baseball players. Therefore, a monopoly element entered into baseball hirings.[2] Baseball teams contended that the reserve clause was essential to the game because it allowed for an even distribution of good players among all teams. It was asserted that without the reserve rules, richer clubs would bid away the best talent. Games would be lopsided, and bored spectators would quit buying tickets.

Although plausible at first glance, this argument loses validity when one realizes that any industry could make a similar statement. In practice, rich firms do not buy up all the best workers and thus make the manufacturing "game" lopsided. Firms and baseball clubs can always borrow money to invest in good workers and good players if the potential payoff for doing so is high enough. Obviously, if only one good (rich) team existed, the payoff from building a competing good team would be high enough to allow a club to borrow money (or sell additional stock) to do so.

[1] Of course it is hard to imagine that a cartel of so many people would actually work. The incentive to cheat would be too great, the problem of inducing new homeowners to join would be large, and the cost of enforcement of the agreement would be tremendous.

[2] The technically correct term is **monopsonist**—one buyer.

Moreover, the value of players depends on gate receipts. How large would ticket sales be with only one good team? Few people would want to see a slaughter at every game involving the best, richest team. Therefore, it behooves good teams to ensure that there are other good teams to compete against in order to generate suspense, excitement, and the resulting higher gate receipts.

The Sherman Antitrust Act, an important piece of **antitrust legislation,** specifically forbids action in restraint of trade, but the Supreme Court ruled in 1922 that owners of baseball teams were exempt from such federal legislation, and its ruling was upheld in 1953 and in 1972. The reserve clause was an attempt to restrict competition among teams for players. As a result, players were making less money than they would have without the clause.

The impact of the reserve clause on players' salaries was, for quite some time, augmented by the effects of a compact between the National and American leagues *not* to compete for each other's players. Such an arrangement would suggest the potential for a third league to bid the best players away from the other two by offering higher salaries. No third U.S. league could have succeeded, however, because players who might have signed with it would be forever barred from the American and National leagues. Apparently not enough players were willing to take this chance, and no other major league appeared.

In an attempt to counter the monopoly power of the baseball team owners, a baseball players' **union** was formed. The union was ultimately successful in its attempts to secure higher salaries for the players and to improve their pension plans. It also succeeded eventually in removing the reserve clause from the players' contracts.

At least up until 1982 (at the writing of this edition), professional football was an almost exact image of what professional baseball used to be. The National Football League (NFL) was the only league in existence from 1919 until 1960, when the American Football League (AFL) appeared. With the appearance of the AFL, players' salaries promptly increased manyfold.

When the NFL ruled the scene, teams could "draft" players

and effectively keep them as long as they wanted. No competition by larger salary offers was allowed. A collusive agreement among NFL team owners prevented players from maximizing their incomes, and no competing league existed to bid players away.

The NFL draft system, which began in 1936, prohibits a college player from negotiating with any professional team other than the one that drafts him. Generally, the worst teams in the league are allowed the first draft choices, presumably to give them a better chance in the forthcoming season.

More than a decade ago, the Washington Redskins drafted star defensive back Jim (Yazoo) Smith. His record at the University of Oregon was impressive, and as a rookie, he was good enough to make the starting lineup for the Redskins. Unfortunately, in the final game of the season, Smith suffered a severe neck injury that ended his career. In September 1976, U.S. Judge William B. Bryant awarded Smith $276,000 in damages—not because of his physical injuries, but because he suffered financial losses. Smith had contended that the league's draft system had restricted his bargaining power with the Redskins, and that the negotiations were so lopsided that he was prevented from obtaining a contract that would have given him financial security when and if he suffered a disabling injury. When the judge struck down the NFL's annual draft of college players, he commented that "this outright, undisguised refusal to deal constitutes a group boycott in its classic and most pernicious form, a device which has long been condemned as per se violation of the antitrust laws." Bryant further added that the draft procedure was "absolutely the most restrictive one imaginable." He also suggested some changes the NFL might make to satisfy the court. For example, three teams might be allowed to choose one player and then bid for that player's services. This, of course, would improve the bargaining position of the players.[3]

---

[3] Note that if no reserve clause existed, the draft system would not work because it would not allocate property rights; without the reserve clause the team owners do not obtain property rights in the players' contracts.

In 1966, after six years of "competition," the AFL and NFL agreed to merge. Congress approved the move as a rider to a public housing bill![4] This merger has affected the freedom of players. Although the terms state that after playing out his contract's one-year option a player may sign with another team, if he does so, the second team must compensate the original team. This, of course, discourages recruitment by the second team. The player can also attempt to arrange a trade through the offices of the football commissioner; however, to date, the results of such negotiations have not been very favorable to the players involved. By precluding the need to compete for players, the AFL-NFL merger has clearly held the salaries of players lower than they would have been under freely competitive conditions.

SUMMARY

Any type of reserve clause in professional sports effectively restricts the ability of team owners to compete for players in an unrestricted sense. The consequence of a reserve clause in a draft system is to reduce players' salaries below what they would be in an unrestricted competitive labor market. A reserve clause in the draft system can only occur when team owners ban together to form a monopoly in the purchasing of players' services. (This type of monopoly is called a monopsony.) Only if the courts continue to allow major league professional team owners to ban together in violation of antitrust laws can such a situation continue.

DISCUSSION QUESTIONS

1. Why is the argument that a reserve clause is necessary to maintain the competitive balance in professional sports invalid, or at least relatively weak?
2. What prevents monopolization in the purchase of inputs (a monopsony) from existing in most labor markets?

[4] This, in spite of a 1967 court ruling that football was subject to antitrust laws.

17

the economics of
Illegal Aliens

Every year about 400,000 persons are legally allowed to immigrate to the United States. Every year at least another million immigrate here illegally. These are the "undocumented aliens," or, more simply, the illegal aliens, who come to this country basically for one reason—better jobs. In 1981 and 1982, about a million illegal aliens a year were stopped by immigration officials, the majority of them at the Mexican border. Some are arrested several times: in fact, one persevering Mexican was arrested five times in one day. The total number of illegal aliens residing in this country is estimated to be somewhere between 5 and 12 million. Certain cities have more than their "fair" share of illegal aliens. Los Angeles, San Diego, and Miami are cases in point. The amount of resources devoted to tracking down illegal aliens and sending them back to their countries of origin has grown rapidly. In fact, according to U.S. House of Representative hearings on the subject, "The number of apprehensions of aliens illegally in the United States appears to be in direct proportion to the number of Immigration and Naturalization Service officers who are available." There is no question about it: illegal aliens seem to be a problem for the United States. This wasn't always so.

Virtually no constraints were placed on immigration into the United States until the 1880s, when convicts, prostitutes, lunatics, and idiots were barred. In 1888, the Act of October 19th called for the deportation of aliens entering this country in violation of the laws. It wasn't until the Immigration Act of 1917, however, that the first systematic arrangement of existing laws on immigration was put into effect. The laws included a literacy requirement, and there were severe restrictions on Orientals. In the Immigration Act of 1924, further restrictions were imposed on immigration from the eastern hemisphere countries, while immigration from the western hemisphere remained unrestricted. By 1965, there was an annual ceiling of 120,000 eastern hemisphere immigrants and 170,000 western hemisphere immigrants.

Historically, then, the United States essentially had an open door policy until the twentieth century. The country continued to grow and prosper throughout virtually all of the period during which its open door policy was in effect. The question now is, Why did public policy seek to change unrestricted immigration if indeed it was associated with growth and continuing improvements in living standards for so many years? To answer it, we must first look at the reason why people wish to immigrate to this country, the effect of their immigration on the labor force, and why Americans used to benefit from it but apparently think they no longer do.

Why do people migrate? Generally speaking, it is for economic reasons. There may have been many social and political reasons why Germans, Swedes, Italians, Scots, Irish, Mexicans, and Chinese wanted to come to America for so many years, but the overriding incentive was economic: they wanted to achieve a higher standard of living.

A decision to migrate on purely economic grounds will be made not only on the basis of potential gain in income, but also of any costs involved in migration. The most obvious (and relatively least important) cost of migration is transportation. After that comes the cost of searching for a job once the immigrant arrives on our shores. This cost can be high if the immigrant is out of work for a long time. Another cost is that of setting up a new household in a different city or country, and dismantling the household one has already created. The costs here are not only economic but also psychic—losing old friends and trying to make new ones, leaving relatives, and so on. All of these costs of migration are incurred at the very beginning, so they loom larger in the immigrant's mind than the potential benefits of the higher wages that he or she may obtain by working in another country. The anticipated stream of differences in wages, then (because that's really what one has to look at), must be compared with the anticipated immigration costs that are incurred almost immediately, but which are generally of a one-time nature.

We can be fairly certain that prior to our restrictive immigration laws, economics was the basis of people's decision to immigrate here. Net immigration into the United States—arrivals minus departures—from the end of the Civil War to the start of World War I dramatically mirrors ups and downs in business activity. During general business depressions, net immigration was low; during general boom times, net immigration grew.

Everything is relative, as we say in economics, and, of course, it is the relative prosperity of America that is important. Thus, the worse off one becomes in one's own country relative to the United States, the more incentive there is to immigrate here. Mexico is a case in point. It has been estimated by the Environmental Fund that Mexico's natural population growth rate is 3.5 percent a year—one of the world's fastest. At such a rate, the number of Mexicans will double in about two decades. At least half of the increase in population is absorbed by illegal immigration into the United States. Presumably, the extra people in Mexico have no place to go. The Mexican National Academy of Economists claims that the ranks of unemployed and underemployed in Mexico are swelling by 800,000 a year; thus, the attractiveness of working in the United States will no doubt become even greater in the future. For a while—from 1942 to 1964—we allowed Mexicans to come into the United States on the "Bracero" Program. At the peak of this program in the 1950s, 400,000 Mexicans worked on farms legally. Of course, once the legal program ended, the number of illegal immigrants increased. This movement of Mexicans into the United States, according to some researchers, may be only the leading edge of a worldwide response to economic disparities. Nobel Prize winner Wassily Leontief referred to this as the "rising, practically irresistible tide of international migration."

Now we must examine why Americans wish to prevent illegal aliens from coming into this country. The basic argument is that they displace American workers from their jobs. But why wasn't this argument always true? To understand the desire of some Americans to keep out foreign workers, we must analyze the impact on our labor market of such immigration. Students familiar with the analysis of the gains from international trade of goods will recognize distinct similarities as we talk about the gains from trade in labor power. In any event, when Mexican workers start crossing the Rio Grande and looking for jobs, they expand the U.S. domestic supply of labor.[1] Given a stable demand curve for labor, wages must fall. Given the existing supply curve before the Mexicans cross the border, we know that at lower wage rates, some Americans will refuse to take jobs. They will indeed be replaced by the Mexican workers. But another thing will happen: U.S. employers looking at the lower wage rate will employ a larger quantity of workers. There will be a higher production of goods and services than before. The ultimate result is, for example, an expansion of potato production in Idaho, lettuce harvesting in California, and avocado raising in Florida. The point is that even though more laborers are working after the Mexicans cross the border, there are fewer domestic workers in the particular labor market. The Mexicans aren't actually throwing the U.S. citizens out of a job. Rather, certain segments of the American labor market face lower wages and, therefore, some of

[1] The supply curve of domestic labor shifts out.

them decide to leave the market. The country may be gaining as a whole, but particular groups of Americans will be the losers. Cesar Chavez, for example, is pro-United Farm Workers, but certainly not pro-Mexican in terms of allowing more legal and illegal aliens into this country.

Also, given that illegal aliens are willing to work at lower wages than U.S. citizens (which is not surprising when one compares the U.S. wage rate they receive to what they would be making in their country of origin), immigration tends to cause previous members of the unskilled labor force to drop out of the labor force and to seek welfare, thus raising the cost of welfare in this country. This problem, however, may be exaggerated. Unemployment rates do indeed seem exceptionally high in places near the Mexican border, such as El Paso and some south Texas counties; but once we move away from border areas, unemployment rates do not seem to be affected by the influx of illegal aliens, at least not in any measurable way. Evidence shows further that few illegal aliens place demands on our publicly provided system of social services. Apparently the cost of the services they do use is exceeded by the amount of money they contribute to federal income taxes and Social Security.

The battle against illegal aliens still rages nonetheless. American workers feel that their jobs are at stake and their salaries in jeopardy. Can the presumably rising tide of illegal immigration be successfully dealt with? Probably not. The illegals are hard to dissuade, for they often flee from bleak job prospects in undesirable living situations. If they are caught in the United States for the first time, it is a misdemeanor punishable by six months in jail and/or a $500 fine. A second time around carries a penalty of two years in jail or a $1000 fine. In actuality, those illegal aliens who are caught are simply sent back to their country of origin. And even that simple job turns out to be phenomenally expensive. The federal government pays the county of Los Angeles $102 per night for each alien's lodging prior to his or her shipment, usually back to Mexico. El Paso, Texas, now spends over $10 million a year for holding illegals in jail prior to deportation.

Politically, two main groups differ over immigration policy. Unions are against immigrants; businesses are for them. It would be virtually impossible to prevent employers from taking advantage of lower-priced, sometimes more productive workers who happen to be illegal aliens. Indeed, most employers using illegals claim they are "better" workers, that is, that they have a higher marginal product. Presumably, this higher marginal product results from their inability to obtain welfare in this country and, hence, their presumably desperate need of work. In short, without a total police state, we won't be able to prevent employers from hiring illegals.

The profit motive for transporting illegals into the United States and protecting them once here has fostered a huge industry. Along the Mexico-California border, smugglers charge anywhere from $50 to $500 to smuggle illegals into the United States. For additional fees, bogus documents can be obtained, including old rent receipts and utility bills. Additionally, many illegals are able to obtain forged work permits.

It's also unrealistic to expect the Mexican government to close off the border. With its rapidly increasing population, Mexico is a labor-intensive country. The United States does not have a rapidly increasing population, and is a capital-intensive country. Mexico can only gain by combining U.S. capital with its labor. Together we produce more goods and services than each of us can independently. It can be viewed as a simple international trade problem. Mexico exports labor services north of the border. The United States pays wages. These are shipped back to Mexico. Eventually, the dollars paid in wages end up being spent by Mexicans on U.S.-produced goods. What we are doing is trading U.S.-made goods for Mexican-provided labor services.

The problem of illegal aliens is here to stay.

SUMMARY

Individuals generally migrate to other countries because of the potential of enjoying a higher standard of living. The proximity of Mexico and other developing countries to the United States guarantees that attempts will be made to enter this country illegally despite laws against such attempts. To the extent that illegal aliens succeed in remaining as workers in the United States, the supply of labor in this country increases (the supply curve shifts outward to the right). Given a stable demand for labor (no equivalent shift in the demand curve), the equilibrium wage rate will necessarily fall, and the quantity of labor demanded will increase. Illegal immigration therefore does not put Americans out of jobs, but reduces relative wage rates in certain low-skilled job categories. It is therefore not hard to understand why unions are in favor of more stringent controls on the entry of illegal aliens into the U.S. labor market.

DISCUSSION QUESTIONS

1. What is one way to completely eliminate the illegal alien problem forever?
2. Why did the U.S. have an open immigration policy for most of its history, but does not have such a policy today?

the economics of
The Big Apple

In our story of the Pernambuco Tramway (Chapter 6), we looked at the immediate problems of setting prices "too low." In this chapter we shall explore other ramifications of setting prices below a market-clearing price. This time we will examine the consequences of rent control in New York City.[1]

Before doing so, it will help to describe briefly the way in which a market adjusts to changes in supply and demand, both in the short and the long run. In this instance, we mean by the short run a period of time too short for the building of new housing units. Now that does not mean that the supply is perfectly inelas-

[1] New York is not alone in its rent control problems. In April 1979, Santa Monica, California, residents voted in Proposition A, which froze rents for 190 days and then was supposed to roll them back to levels of April 1978. If Santa Monica rent control is truly effective, that city will eventually face problems similar to those experienced in New York.

tic. Why not? Because a higher price for housing will encourage people who own homes or housing units to rent part of their units rather than keep them all for themselves. There is, therefore, some short-run elasticity of supply. A shift in demand, reflecting, as it did in New York during World War II, a sudden increase of people seeking apartments, would lead to a sharp rise in price and some increase in the quantity of units available.

The consequence, in the long run, is to set in motion the forces that make for a new equilibrium, which is essentially the way a market system works. A sharp rise in the price of apartments makes it attractive for entrepreneurs to invest their money in building new housing. To put it another way, the rate of return to investing in the housing stock has increased as compared to other ways an entrepreneur could use his or her capital. This results in new construction, which in turn leads to a downward movement in the price of housing as the supply increases, until ultimately an equilibrium is reached. Note that the implication is that the long-run supply of housing is relatively elastic under free market conditions, in contrast to the short run. The long-run equilibrium is one in which the rate of return on investing in one more unit of housing is just equal to that of investing in any other similar economic activity with the same degree of risk.

Now back to our story of New York. In 1943, the federal government imposed rent control as a temporary wartime measure. While the federal program ended after the war, it was continued in New York State, and specifically in New York City. The law in the city kept rent for certain categories of apartments at fixed levels, allowing a 15 percent increase when a tenant moved out. Needless to say, an immediate consequence was that landlords tended to encourage such departures by everything from pounding on the pipes to cutting off the heat. Since there were many more people seeking apartments than there were apartments available, a longer-run consequence was the development of a vast array of devices to attempt to get around the restrictions. The most obvious was what was called key money, which was a way to charge a prospective renter a large amount of money simply to get the key to an apartment; or one could hire the landlord's son to repaint the apartment at a substantial fee. In other cases, the landlord would discriminate among prospective tenants on the basis of race, religion, dogs, children, or whatever. Still another consequence was that landlords simply failed to maintain apartments, so that their real costs of upkeep were decreased.

All of these policies suggest that landlords and tenants were simply finding a way to get around the artificially low price and in fact develop a de facto equilibrium. That is, the real value of apartments fell and/or the tenant in fact paid an extra price. Thus, in reality, shifts in the supply and demand curves occurred.

One obvious consequence of rent control was widespread evasion of the law. Laws were passed in an attempt to force landlords to maintain apartments, but these were widely evaded. Other laws were designed to prevent subletting for higher prices. These, too, were widely evaded, so much so that a 1960 survey showed that 25 percent of renters were paying more than the legal price for rent-controlled apartments. Note that this did not include bribes or cuts in quality. These were simply people paying above the amount stipulated. We observe that in such circumstances the market does find its own equilibrium.

Nevertheless, rent control has significant consequences for both renter and landlord. Clearly, a landlord suffers in terms of drop in income and a renter suffers in terms of a quality reduction in apartments. However, that is not the end of the story. As of 1975, some 642,000 apartments were rent-controlled. Another 650,000 were covered by a complex form of regulation called rent stabilization. During the whole period since World War II, there has been almost no construction of apartments that would be subject to rent control. Moreover, apartments deteriorated because it was not worthwhile for landlords to keep them up; eventually the annual taxes on the apartment houses exceeded the income the landlord received, and the apartments were simply abandoned. In 1970, 33,000 housing units were abandoned. As late as 1974, 10,000 more were abandoned. In some parts of the Bronx and on Manhattan's lower East Side, whole rows of abandoned apartment houses stood gutted and stripped by vandals.

Thus, the long-run consequences in New York City have been a decay in the housing stock and a decline in the amount of available space for middle- and lower-income tenants (luxury apartments, exempted from rent control, have continued to be built). But there have been more serious consequences: the tax base of New York has been primarily housing real estate, and as this base eroded, New York's fiscal income declined.

The result, as we all know, has been a city perched on the edge of bankruptcy. According to fiscal experts, in spite of promises, government guarantees, and refinancing of the debt *ad nauseum*, the Big Apple is still spending more than it is taking in.

SUMMARY

Each production activity requires factors of production. Use of those factors of production will continue as long as at least a normal rate of return can be obtained. The provision of housing services is no different than the provision of any other product or service—it requires factors of production. Rent controls restrict the ability of landlords to charge a market-clearing price. To the extent that rent controls are effective, they can lead to a reduction in the current quality of housing services available, as well as a reduction in the future supply of housing services. Investors who cannot make a normal rate of return will no longer choose to invest in apartment buildings. Therefore, rent controls can have a short-run effect and a long-run effect. Both effects have a negative impact on many individuals seeking "affordable" housing.

DISCUSSION QUESTIONS

1. Who benefits from rent controls in the short run? In the long run?
2. Why would any landlord ever completely abandon an apartment building?

the economics of
Minimum Wages

In an unrestricted labor market, there will be an equilibrium wage rate at which the quantity of labor demanded will equal the quantity supplied. In essence, any analysis of labor markets is equivalent to the supply-demand analysis for any product sold. The analysis of **minimum wage** legislation is similar to the analysis of any restriction on the market price for a particular product. If we look at employment in different industries and among different groups of individuals, we find that certain industries and some specific groups in the labor force seem to consistently experience unusually high rates of unemployment. For example, teenagers—black teenagers in particular—have for many years now experienced rates of unemployment two and three times those of other subgroups in the labor force. To understand why different groups experience differential rates of unemployment, we must look at the history and effect of minimum wage legislation.

At the turn of the century, minimum wage legislation grew out of the general movement against the "exploitation of the poor working girl" and the low pay for workers toiling in what were then considered bad working conditions, or "sweatshops." By 1913, seven states had imposed compulsory minimum wage rates applicable to women and minors. During President Roosevelt's New Deal, a federal minimum wage was set as part of the National Industrial Recovery Act. However, the NIRA was declared unconstitutional by the Supreme Court in 1937 and so, too, were the minimum wages established under it. Within a year, though, the Fair Labor Standards Act was passed, which established a minimum wage of 25 cents for all industries involved in interstate commerce. This act has remained the basis for all federal minimum wage legislation. Since that time, minimum wages have gradually increased to their current level.

To analyze the effects of any kind of minimum wage legislation, we must first answer this question: What determines the wage rate that workers are paid in the absence of restrictions? Basically, in the aggregate, employers will hire workers up to the point where the value of the additional output made possible by the new worker just equals the increase in the employer's wage bill. In other words, on the margin, workers are paid what they are worth to the employer.[1] When a wage rate is arbitrarily increased, some marginal workers become unprofitable to employ. Given a constant **aggregate demand,** a higher wage rate imposed by a government-legislated minimum wage means that some employers can no longer afford to employ those marginal workers because the market value of their contribution to total output is less than the minimum wage.

Workers who lose their jobs, who are not rehired, or who cannot find jobs at the minimum wage receive no wage at all. They must find jobs in sectors of the economy that are not covered by minimum wage legislation. But to induce employers in these other sectors to take on additional workers, wage rates in these sectors must, by necessity, fall. Hence, by eliminating mar-

---

[1] The wage rate equals the **value of marginal product.**

ginal job opportunities in industries it covers, the minimum wage hurts some of the very people it was intended to help.

True, a change of a few cents in the minimum wage may not greatly affect the total employment picture. However, consider what happened in 1956 when the minimum wage jumped from 75 cents to $1 an hour, an increase of one-third. A few years later, the Secretary of Labor concluded in a report that "there were significant declines in employment in most of the low-wage industries studied."

Which group of workers constitutes "marginal" workers? Those with the least experience and the least amount of training and education—in other words, the teenage labor force. Teenagers generally have the lowest productivity in the economy. Indeed, it is by working on a low-paid job that teenagers can increase their productivity and hence their future income potential. The data bear out our prediction that they would be most affected by the minimum wage. In 1956, when there was a one-third jump in the minimum wage, nonwhite teenage unemployment increased from 13 percent to more than 24 percent! A 1965 study by Arthur Burns concluded that "the ratio of the unemployment rate of teenagers to that of male adults was invariably higher during the six months following an increase in the minimum wage than it was in the preceding half year."

Increases in the minimum wage have another effect that is perhaps less well known. They increase the demand[2] for other types of workers, that is, for substitute workers or, more specifically, higher-skilled, higher-paid union workers. We can assume that a certain amount of substitution is possible between union workers and nonunion workers, even though the latter are generally less skilled, particularly those among them who may be affected by minimum wage legislation. At a low enough price, an employer will find it profitable to hire more lower-skilled nonunion workers in the place of fewer higher-skilled and higher-paid union workers. However, as the relative price of nonunion, lower-skilled workers rises, the employer finds it less advanta-

[2] The demand schedule shifts (outward) to the right.

geous to hire them in place of the more expensive union workers. It is not surprising, therefore, that the strongest supporters of increases in the minimum wage are unions and members of Congress representing states that are heavily unionized, particularly in the North.

The effects of a minimum wage law depend crucially upon whether or not it is enforced. If the law is not enforced, it may have no effect whatsoever. The analysis of minimum wages is identical to the analysis of price controls. Although it is easy to analyze the effects of minimum wage legislation, because the law spells out specifically which kinds of labor are covered and what exemptions are allowed, it does not always follow that the minimum wage is effective.

There are ways to circumvent minimum wage laws. In every instance where low-paid workers are receiving benefits in kind, such as below-cost lunches or free tickets to professional football games, there can be a substitution of increases in money wages for benefits in kind. For example, if a minimum wage forces money wages to go up, the employer can raise the price of lunches or charge for professional football tickets to make up the difference between the new minimum wage and the former lower-wage rate. Furthermore, firms may require kickbacks from employees, establish company stores, or require workers to live in company-owned housing. The new prices for company-store products or company-owned housing may now exceed their market value. This amounts to paying a lower wage. If a minimum wage is forced on the employer, the actual wage can still be kept below the legal minimum by use of these devices.

Another method to avoid the minimum wage loss is to hire relatives. In many cases, relatives of employers, particularly close relatives, are not covered under minimum wage laws and/ or are not monitored closely by the Department of Labor. This way of avoiding minimum wage laws may be a clue to understanding how small neighborhood grocery stores and restaurants can successfully compete with larger, presumably more efficient enterprises in their area. Dry-cleaning establishments owned by retired couples apparently are competing very effectively with the larger dry-cleaning chains, presumably because of the former's ability to avoid minimum wage legislation. (The owners of the firm don't have to pay themselves any particular wage rate.)

We also must be careful to distinguish between the short run and the long run. It is a general proposition that short-run curves tend to be less elastic than long-run curves. Hence, we would expect the minimum wage to have a much smaller effect in the short run than in the long run. What we need to know (in order to assess its full impact on employment) is what happens in the long run.

The most recent research on the effect of minimum wages indicates that minimum wage legislation weakens the economic status of those at the bottom of the distribution of earnings. The apparent redistribution of income that occurs as a result of the minimum wage appears to be from some "have nots" to other "have nots." Additionally, the most skilled low-wage workers are the very ones who are not put out of work by increases in the minimum wage rate. The poorest group—workers who are likely to be the least productive—are the most likely to become unemployed as a result of minimum wage rate increases.

SUMMARY

To the extent that minimum wage legislation is effectively enforced, it reduces employment possibilities for individuals whose productivity is such that the value of their marginal product is less than the legislated minimum wage. Minimum wage legislation therefore creates unemployment for the relatively untrained and unskilled—teenagers, members of minorities, the very old.

DISCUSSION QUESTIONS

1. What effect does inflation have on our minimum wage analysis?
2. What are some of the ways that employers can avoid paying minimum wages?
3. Despite the above arguments, make the best case you can in favor of minimum wage legislation.

20

the economics of
Crime Prevention

In 1981, New York City chose to permit 1832 murders, 3862 rapes, 107,495 robberies, 207,931 burglaries, and 26,775 assaults, as well as various numbers of lesser crimes.

Stated in other terms, New York City appropriated a sum in excess of $669 million for the police department for that year. We start our examination with an assumption that the amount of resources devoted to crime prevention is inversely related to the amount of crime. Had the city of New York appropriated twice that amount, would there have been less crime? How much less? In short, what is the relation between prevention of crime and money spent? How did the city decide on that figure?

Before we can begin to answer these questions, we must look in greater detail at the economics of fighting crime. First of all, it is not just the police and other law-enforcement agencies that are involved in crime prevention. The courts and various types of penal and reform institutions also enter the picture, as do devices such as burglar alarms, locks, and safes. In total, more than $147 billion was spent to combat crime in the United States in 1981 (about 4 percent of net national product).

Law enforcement has many aspects and the costs of each must be considered in allocating the resources available. The costs can be divided into three general areas. First there are the costs of the crime detection (in cases such as narcotics or prostitution) and the arrest of suspects. Second, costs are involved in the trial and conviction of the prisoner; they vary with the efficiency and speed with which the law-enforcement officials and the courts can act. Third, once sentence is imposed, there are the economic costs of maintaining and staffing prisons. This third area, and the social implications of the question: What sorts and durations of punishment are most effective as deterrents to crime? will be examined in Chapter 28.

As noted above, the amount of resources devoted to discovering and apprehending criminals is related to a reduction in crime. But the optimum allocation of those resources is not so clear-cut. The chief of police or the commissioner is faced with two sets of problems. On the one hand, this individual must decide how to divide the funds between capital and labor—that is, choose between more cars, equipment, and laboratories, or more police personnel, detectives, and technicians. On the other hand, he or she must also allocate funds among the various police details within the department, for example, decide whether to clamp down harder on homicide or on car theft.

Within a law-enforcement budget of a given size, the police chief must then determine the optimum combination of production factors. The ideal combination is one in which an additional dollar spent on any one of the labor or capital inputs will provide an equal additional amount of enforcement. If an additional dollar spent on laboratory equipment yields a higher crime-deterrent result than the same dollar spent on a police officer's salary, the laboratory will win. While it is clear that inputs cannot be measured in such small amounts, the question of *indivisibility*,[1] or lumpiness in production, does not alter the basic argument. Nor does it alter the argument that we cannot precisely measure the returns on an increase in labor or in some input of **capital**. The police captain must normally judge from experience and intuition, as well as from available data, whether buying more cars or hiring more men and women will do the better job in checking crime. And note that this decision may change with changes in relative price. For example, when the salaries of police officers are raised, the balance may tip toward the use of more cars or equipment, depending on how well capital can be substituted for labor in a given situation. Instead of using two police officers in a car, it might be economically efficient to equip the car with bulletproof glass and let the driver patrol alone.

The second task of the police chief is to determine how to allocate resources among the interdepartmental details. Sometimes highly publicized events may influence this decision. For example, a few years ago, prostitution increased in downtown Seattle to such a degree that local merchants protested vigorously that streetwalkers were hurting business. They had sufficient political influence to induce the police chief to step up sharply the detection and apprehension of prostitutes. That meant using more personnel and equipment on the vice squad; and within the restriction of a fixed budget this could be done only by pulling resources away from homicide, robbery, and other details, which were thus made short-handed. In effect, the cost of reducing prostitution was a short-run increase in assault and robbery. It is not clear (in the short run, at least) that political pressure of the sort just mentioned leads to a concentration of police enforcement in those areas that many people feel are most essential.

We said that three general areas of law enforcement entail costs to society, and we have just dealt with the area of detection and arrest. The second area is the trial and its outcome. Recent

[1] A good or service is said to be indivisible if it can be sold only in relatively large quantities. For example, one cannot purchase one-tenth of a police car. However, perhaps the car can be rented for one-tenth of each month. Given the possibility of rental, many products can no longer be called indivisible.

studies indicate that the likelihood of conviction is a highly important factor (if not the major one) in the prevention of crime. Currently, the probability of conviction and punishment for crime is extremely low in the United States. In New York City, it is estimated that an individual who commits a felony faces less than 1 chance in 200 of going to jail.[2] Poor crime detection partly explains this incredible figure; court congestion adds to the problem. In highly urbanized environments, the court calendar is so clogged that the delay in getting a case to trial may stretch from months into years.[3] One consequence of this situation is an increasing tendency for the prosecutor and suspect to arrange a pretrial settlement rather than further overburden the courts. This is what happens to 80–90 percent of criminal charges. The effect on the morale of the police officers who have brought the cases to trial is obvious. Society may be underinvesting in the resources necessary to improve this process. If more were to be spent on streamlining court proceedings instead of on making arrests, cases could be brought to trial more promptly, the presence of all witnesses could be more easily secured, and the hand of the D.A. would not be forced in making "deals" with suspects. Faced with the probability of quick and efficient trial, a potential criminal might think harder about robbing a bank or mugging a pedestrian. Chief Justice Warren E. Burger himself has recently declared that we do in fact need an overhauling of our courts.

There remains another issue which is highly controversial. The likelihood of detection and conviction can be increased by new technical means, by wiretapping, and by changes in the laws protecting the rights of suspects (e.g., permitting law officers to enter and search without knocking, lifting the requirement that suspects be informed of their constitutional rights, and allowing the holding of suspects incommunicado for lengthy periods). However, the consequences of such legal changes in terms of infringement on individual liberties are extremely serious, and in

[2] *Wall Street Journal*, August 20, 1970.
[3] Many court calendars are solidly booked for two, three, or even five years into the future. In New York, for example, the average time lapse between filing a civil suit and getting it to trial is 39 months.

any event we do not have the information necessary to determine how effective such changes would be.

We can now return to our original question. How did New York City determine that a budget for crime prevention in excess of $669 million was the right amount? In the short run, the city was faced with a total budget of a given size and had to decide how to carve it up between law enforcement and other municipal demands, such as fire protection, health, parks, streets, and libraries. Just as a police chief may try to determine what combination of police officers and equipment within his or her fixed budget will deter the greatest amount of crime, a city council will attempt to choose a combination of spending on all agencies that will yield the maximum amount of public services. If additional money spent on fire protection does not yield as much "good" as it would if spent on police protection, then the amount should be allocated to law enforcement.[4] Determining the value of services rendered by each agency poses a touchy problem. However, the problem is not insuperable, at least in principle. We will see in the case of the Hell's Canyon issue (Chapter 23) that crude approximations can be made of the benefits and costs of recreation. This applies equally to other nonpriced goods and services, and the efficiency of the public sector of our economy will be improved as such calculations are made and refined.

The short-run constraint of a fixed budget for law enforcement may be altered in the long run by going to the state legislature and asking for increased funds for crime prevention. The legislature will then have to wrestle with the same allocation problem that engaged the city council. Funds can be increased for a city's budget only by tightening the belt in some other area, such as school expenditures or park development. The same, familiar calculations must also be made on the state level: Will spending an additional dollar on higher education yield greater returns for society than the same dollar given to a city council to allocate to crime prevention? The same difficult question arises in

---

[4] The city council equates on the margin returns from money spent on all municipal activities.

measuring the dollar value of nonpriced services resulting from any given state expenditure.

The state does have an option not open to most city councils in most states: it can raise taxes. If it chooses to, this will widen the allocation problem. The increased taxes will reduce the disposable income of some part of the citizenry. Those who pay the additional taxes must in turn decide whether they feel the additional public services made available are worthwhile. For example, is the reduction in crime attributable to an increased expenditure on law enforcement as valuable to them as the goods they could have enjoyed from that increased tax money? If they do not think so, then at the next election they will vote to "throw the rascals out."

The above description indicates that nonmarket solutions to economic problems run basically parallel to market solutions. Although we have focused on crime prevention, the criteria are similar for all types of government decisions and for all levels of government—local, state, and federal.

But certain differences must also be noted between decision making in the private market sector of the economy and in the public nonmarket sector. Problems of measurement are much greater in the latter. How, for example, do we put a price tag on recreation, which is the output of the parks department? And the signals come through much louder and more clearly in market situations, in which changes in private profitability "telegraph" to entrepreneurs what policies will be best.[5] Instead of market signals, makers of public policy receive a confused set of noises generated by opponents and proponents of their decisions. A legislator is in the unenviable position of trying to please as many of the electorate as possible while operating with very incomplete information.

Some cities have tried to use market mechanisms to improve crime prevention. A few years ago, the city of Orange, California, near Los Angeles, started paying its police according

---

[5] In instances where **externalities** exist, it may be to society's advantage to alter these signals by appropriate measures.

to how much crime was reduced. The incentive scheme applied to four categories of crime—burglary, robbery, rape, and auto theft. Under the plan, as first put into effect, if the crime rate in those categories was cut by 3 percent for the first eight months of the year compared with the first eight months in the previous year, the police would get an extra 1-percent raise. If the crime rate fell by 6 percent, the pay increase would be an extra 2 percent. The results have been encouraging. Detectives on their own time produce videotape briefings with leads for patrol officers on specific beats. The whole force developed a campaign to encourage safety precautions in residents' homes. Statistically speaking, the results were even more impressive, for during the first seven months of the program crime in the four categories listed above fell by 17.62 percent. The other crime figures held steady, indicating that the police force was not merely shifting its efforts from one area of crime to another.

On the basic question of the allocation of resources within a police department or within a municipality, there is a way in which such allocation might be altered. Right now, in many cities and states of the Union, a person beaten up in the streets and left with permanent brain damage cannot sue for injuries. The attacker, if caught, will be jailed. That does not help the victim, who ends up paying taxes for the prisoner's room and board!

But if the city or state were held liable for all damages sustained, the victim (or dependents) could sue the city or state for compensation. Unlimited liability on the part of government for crimes against the populace would certainly alter the present allocation of resources between crime prevention and other public endeavors.

On June 8, 1982, an initiative was passed in California which was widely referred to as a "bill of rights" for crime victims. It required convicts to make restitution to those harmed (it also made other broad changes such as putting limits on bail releases and insanity pleas). Now approximately three-fifths of the states have established funds to compensate crime victims. But for the most part, the compensation is far less than the full cost of the crime. What if a state were obligated for the full cost of a crime committed within its borders? How would that affect the expenditure on crime prevention?

This raises the question of what lawyers call "moral hazard." If victims of robberies, for example, were fully compensated by the municipality, there would be less incentive for individuals to protect themselves privately against robberies. The same is true for other crimes. One way to avoid this "moral hazard" is to establish a deductible on the municipality's liability. For example, for home robberies, the municipality might be held responsible for all losses in excess of $500. If this were the case, homeowners still would have an incentive to lock their doors, have watchdogs, and keep lights on at night when they are away.

Crime costs. So does crime prevention. But the latter has benefits to society that should be weighed when making decisions about law-enforcement methods and expenditures.

SUMMARY

If we consider crime prevention the output of the police force, then the inputs used are labor and capital. The capital consists of squad cars, computers, surveillance equipment, and the like. If a law enforcement agency were operated as a profit-seeking business, it would utilize a mix of labor and machines such that the last dollar spent on each would yield the same marginal product. One of the difficulties in analyzing the mix of crime prevention resources as they apply to different types of crimes is that the value of the output is often unknown. That is to say, no one can objectively say that the prevention of a robbery is more desirable than the prevention of an illicit drug transaction.

DISCUSSION QUESTIONS

1. Discuss the allocation of resources of other nonmarket activities, such as higher education, firefighting, or highway construction.
2. How does a firm decide how to allocate resources? How does it differ from a government agency?

part four

Social Issues and Externalities

INTRODUCTION

Many issues in our society do not seem to lend themselves to strict supply-demand analysis. Typically these issues involve what are called *externalities*, that is, either the costs or the benefits —or both—of some economic activity are external to the decision-making process of those who are generating them. An example of a negative externality is air pollution. Externalities, whether they be negative or positive, typically occur because of a common property problem. Common property is property that at one and the same time is owned by no one and by everyone. Air and, to a lesser extent, water have been treated as common property for many years. Since no one effectively owns common property, no one has an incentive to efficiently use (or not abuse) it.

The lack of property rights is the central issue in the chapters on animal extinction, clamming, oil spills, flooding Hell's Canyon, and auto congestion. These are all social issues involving social costs and benefits.

An explicit attempt to create property rights in the ability to pollute is discussed in Chapter 27, while Chapter 28 deals with the concept of overpollution and that of running out of resources.

All of the issues discussed in this part demonstrate the power of economic analysis. Social issues have a way of becoming economic issues, because they typically involve decisions about how to use scarce resources.

21

the economics of
Animal Extinction

In its report on the Endangered Species Act of 1973, the Senate Commerce Committee concluded that the two major causes of animal extinction are hunting and destruction of habitat. There is certainly an element of truth in this observation: ever since prehistoric times humans and animals have competed for space and habitat on this planet. The problem, however, is more complex than a simple statement of that sort.

Let us begin with prehistoric times. The destruction of animal species by humans is nothing new. The arrival of human beings in North America about 12,000 years ago is usually tied to the extinction of most of the existing megafauna. The LaBrea Tarpits yielded 24 mammals and 22 birds which no longer exist. Among these are the saber tooth tiger, the giant llama, the 20-foot ground sloth, a bison that stands 7 feet at the hump with 6-foot wide horns, etc.

In fact, only 0.02 percent of all of the species that have ever existed on earth are currently extant. While many believe that human hunting was directly responsible for the destruction of these species, there is some evidence to the contrary.

The argument for direct human guilt in destroying these animals is based on the view that humans were indiscriminate, wasteful hunters. Hunting methods such as driving animals over a cliff, which resulted in many more being killed than could be used by the tribe, are illustrations of this indiscriminate destruction of male and female animals alike. The fact that no group had exclusive property rights over animals meant that there was no incentive to husband the resource. If one group was careful and husbanded the animals, another group would simply exploit them in competition with that group.

This view has not gone unchallenged. Some have argued that, in fact, primitive tribes did husband the resource and attempted to kill off only the weaker animals, saving the females of the species. But note that the issue was still one over property rights. To the degree that the animals were exclusively within the hunting range of only one tribe, that tribe had an incentive to husband the resource and to provide for a perpetual renewal of those animals.

Whether or not primitive tribes in America were responsible for the extinction of many early animals and birds is still an open question; but the role of human beings in the extinction of animals at a later time is much clearer. The first known instance is the extinction of the European lion, the last survivor being dated in A.D. 80. In modern times the most famous example is that of the passenger pigeon. At one time these birds were the most numerous species of birds in North America and perhaps in the world. They nested and migrated together in huge flocks, and may have numbered more than a billion. When flocks passed overhead the sky would be dark with pigeons, literally for days at a time. Audubon measured one roost at 40 miles long and about 3 miles wide. While the Indians had long hunted these birds, it was the arrival of the white man and the demand for pigeons as a food source that led to their ultimate demise. The birds were netted in vast numbers. And by the end of the nineteenth century, an animal species which had been looked upon as literally indestructible because of its enormous numbers had almost completely disappeared. The last known passenger pigeon died in the Cincinnati zoo in 1914.

The American bison only narrowly escaped the same fate. The vast herds that roamed the plains were an easy target for hunters; with the advent of the railroad and the need to feed railroad crews as transcontinental railroad lines were built, hunters like Buffalo Bill Cody killed bison by the thousands. Then as the demand for the fur of the bison increased, it became the target for still further hunting. Like the passenger pigeon, the bison appeared to be indestructible because of its numbers. But in the absence of any property rights over bison, the result was almost the same as with the passenger pigeon—bison were becoming extinct. Despite the outcries of the Indians who found their major food source being decimated, it was not until late in the nineteenth century that any efforts were made to protect the bison.

The fate of the passenger pigeon and of the bison illustrates the main dilemma of protecting endangered species. To the degree that there are no ownership rights over these animals, anyone can attempt to hunt them for private gain. The conflict between the needs of human beings for food or clothing and the survival of a particular species can only lead to one end—the extinction of the animal species.

In modern times, government has attempted, by means of state and federal regulation, to limit hunting seasons and the number of animals or birds that may be taken. The results have been at least partially successful. It is probable that there are more deer in North America today than there were at the time of the colonists. The same is true for a number of other animal species. In effect, a rationing system (rather than prices) was used to limit the exploitation of a "common property resource." But the threatened extinction in modern times of many species of whales illustrates that the problem is far from resolved.

The pattern of harvesting whales has been the subject of international discussion ever since World War II; it was readily apparent to all concerned that without some form of restraint, the whaling population was in danger of extinction. The result was the setting up of an international regulatory body, the International Whaling Commission (IWC), in 1948, in an attempt to regulate international whaling through cooperative endeavor. But the IWC was virtually doomed from the start. Its members were given the right to veto any regulation they considered too restrictive; if a member decided to blatantly disobey regulations, the IWC had no enforcement powers. Since some whaling nations, such as Chile and Peru, refused to join the IWC, quotas had little effect on these nations. And some IWC members have used nonmember flagships to circumvent the quotas themselves.

The story of the decimation of a species is probably best told in the events surrounding the blue whale. Even with the most modern equipment, the great blue whale, which sometimes weighs almost a hundred tons, is difficult to kill; but intensive hunting methods gradually reduced the stock from somewhere between 300,000 and 1,000,000 to, at present, somewhere between 600 and 3000. In the 1930–1931 winter season almost 30,000 blue whales were taken. By 1945–1946, less than 10,000 were taken; and in the late 1950s the yearly catch was down to around 1500 per year. By 1964–1965, the total was only 20 whales. In 1965, a ban was placed by the IWC on killing blue whales. But even after the ban, the hunting of blues continued from land stations by nonmembers such as Brazil, Chile, and Peru.

Humpback whales have suffered a similar fate. From an original population estimated at 300,000, there remain between 1500 and 5000 today. Like the blues, humpbacks are now under a hunting ban, but the lack of monitoring capacity makes it probable that the ban is only nominal. The problems of the IWC can be seen in the reactions to several conservation measures passed at the 1973 meeting. The United States pushed through measures banning the hunting of finbacks in the Antarctic, setting the quota on minke whales at 5000 instead of 12,000 as Japan requested, and instituting an area by area quota for sperm whales so that the total population would be protected. A year later, the

Japanese and then the Russians, parties to these agreements, announced they would set more realistic quotas in line with Japanese interests.

Moreover, even where government regulations attempt to protect animals, poaching, a lucrative source of income, has been widespread. This is particularly true in poor nations: to an individual native hunter in Africa, the income from the ivory tusks of a single elephant may be the difference between starvation and relative abundance.

Nothing better illustrates the dilemma of animal extinction than the cases of the snail darter and of the coyote. The National Environmental Policy Act of 1969 made it mandatory that an environmental impact statement be made on all projects which would affect the environment. A mechanism was thus created for the protection of endangered species against environmental destruction. The most famous example involves the snail darter, a small fish whose existence was threatened by the construction of a dam proposed by the Tennessee Valley Authority (TVA). The environmental impact statement process required the TVA to list the extinction of the snail darter as the probable outcome of the construction of the dam. The 1973 Endangered Species Act, with its clause requiring emergency action to protect any species threatened with extinction, was invoked. The result was a national furor in which the benefits to humankind of the additional power to be provided by the dam were measured against the possible extinction of an obscure small fish, the existence of which was known only to a very small number of people. In fact, this issue was resolved when the TVA reevaluated the benefit costs of the dam and concluded that it was not worthwhile after all. Nevertheless, many people viewed the conflict as an absurd one in terms of the benefit costs of a snail darter versus hydroelectric power.

However, if the snail darter illustrates an absurdity in the efforts to save animals from extinction, the case of coyote versus sheep highlights a more difficult dilemma. The coyote has not come under protection, but the ways by which it can be hunted have been severely limited; in particular, some methods of poisoning the coyote have been restricted or forbidden, with the result that there has been an enormous growth in their population.

Lamb is a favorite food of the coyote. Consequently, the sheepherders in many areas have found it prohibitively expensive to raise sheep because of their ravaging by a growing coyote population. With fewer sheep, the relative prices of wool and lamb have risen significantly in the United States. What should be the outcome? Should the coyote be protected, as many environmental groups have insisted, and are we willing to pay the price of substantially higher costs for wool and lamb as a result? The conflict between man and animal species is not easily resolved, as these two cases illustrate.

SUMMARY

If one were to draw up two separate lists of animals—those that are endangered and those that are not—one would be hard-pressed to come up with a single set of physical characteristics distinguishing the two. In actuality, the main distinction between endangered animals and nonendangered ones is that the former are common property. There is no incentive for a single individual to refrain from killing common property animals, because the action will have no effect on the total number of animals that ultimately survive. All of the government restrictions on hunting are an attempt to overcome the common property problem. Unfortunately, even government restrictions are hard to enforce in the case of animals that are constantly on the move, such as the whale.

DISCUSSION QUESTIONS

1. Has there ever been a problem of the extinction of dogs, cats, or cattle? Why not?
2. Some argue that the only way to save rare species is to set up private game reserves to which wealthy hunters can travel. How could this help save endangered species?

22

the economics of
Oil Spills

On March 1, 1978, the registered tanker, the Amoco Cadiz, encountered huge seas off the Brittany coast of France. Apparently its captain waited too late to call for help. The tanker split apart, sending 54.6 million gallons of oil into the sea. Estimated damage to French fishermen, land owners, tourists, business owners, and others ran into the billions of dollars.

 This disaster followed ten years of smaller but still important oil spills. In March 1967, the oil tanker Torrey Canyon foundered off the southern coast of England and spilled 119,000 tons of crude oil. At that time, such an amount was considered a phenomenal problem. Even though the British government alone spent $8 million on clean-up, the oil slick stayed on the waters of English and French coasts for some time. Then, just as with the Amoco Cadiz, people were made aware of the threat posed by modern tankers with capacities ranging in excess of a million tons. The size of these ships is mind-boggling and the amount of oil they carry awesome. Since most ships are typically fueled by oil, the threat of spillage is not limited to tank ships and barges. In addition to accidents, spills can result from leaks in transferring oil, from the deliberate pumping out of bilges, and from blowouts of offshore wells, as in the Santa Barbara case.[1] In 1974 there were 26 major oil spills (11 in U.S. waters), topped off by the supertanker Metulla off the southern tip of South America with a spill of 26 million gallons of oil. Since oil is not biodegradable (does not deteriorate rapidly), the oceans of the world are accumulating an ever-increasing mass of "indigestible" petroleum; slicks and globules of oil are visible on the high seas all over the world. The biological consequences are still indeterminate — we simply do not know what the long-run effects on marine life will be. But anybody who has walked the beaches barefoot is aware of the fouling consequences of oil on coastlines.

Moreover, the problem is complicated by the crisis in petroleum supplies that has resulted from the successful cartel activities of the oil-exporting countries (see Chapter 1). The price of oil rose from approximately $3 a barrel before the Yom Kippur War of 1973 to over $11 in 1976. In 1982, the price per barrel was $32.42. Predictably, the result of this price increase has been to encourage new sources of supply, particularly offshore drilling, to complete the construction of a pipeline across Alaska for North Slope oil, and to encourage even more giant tankers to bring in oil. Already a major controversy has emerged over the transporting of North Slope oil to markets. Should it be brought by tanker through the Straits of Juan de Fuca and into Puget Sound? A spill from a supertanker in those confined waters would be a major disaster to the region.

Some technological methods have already been evolved for cleaning up the oil mess, and better ones may be devised in the

---

[1] The focus of this chapter is on oil spills directly into water. An additional problem is posed by oil spills on land — intentional or accidental — from pipelines, disposal of used oil from 230,000 gasoline stations, etc. Eventually such oil seeps into streams, rivers, lakes, and oceans.

future. But it may prove far less costly to society to prevent future spills effectively. Several alternatives can be considered.

One proposed solution is simply to prohibit offshore drilling and the transportation of petroleum products by water. This would certainly reduce oil spills, but it might lead to undesirable side effects for various sectors of the community. The short-run effects would be a reduction in the supply of crude oil and a resultant rise in the price of all petroleum products. Rich and poor alike use gasoline, but it represents a larger proportion of the expenditures of the poor.[2] Hence, a greater burden would fall on low-income groups. The long-run consequences of such a policy are somewhat more difficult to determine. A rise in the price of petroleum products would increase the profitability of new domestic discoveries and thereby lead to more intensive exploration. Whether this would sufficiently increase the supply to cause the price to fall to earlier levels is doubtful.

Moreover, even if such a drastic measure were taken by the United States, it would not completely solve the problem, because others nations' tankers would still carry oil and continue to foul the oceans. Since our legal authority extends only a short distance out to sea, our beaches would still not be safe from wandering oil slicks.

It is possible to eliminate most ecological problems by simply shutting off any economic activity that has costs to "innocent bystanders." But this is usually a prohibitively expensive solution. The number of economic activities with external diseconomies is constantly growing, and totally forbidding such activities would result in a drastic fall in living standards. Can we, then, eliminate the bulk of these side effects without eliminating the economic activity that produces them? These baneful effects exist for one reason: the individuals or groups who create the costs do not bear even a small fraction of them. If the polluters

[2] Studies have shown the following distribution of gasoline expenditures as a proportion of income: $3000–$5000 income, 3.4 percent; $5000–$7000 income, 3.3 percent; $7000–$15000 income, less than 2 percent; above $15,000, 1.4 percent.

had to bear the full social costs, it would be in their interest to eliminate as many of the effects as is economic. [3]

In short, one pat answer to most pollution questions is to make the polluter pay. But to do so, we would have to alter property rights—that is, change existing laws about ownership. Rights to property would have to be revised to include the costs as well as the benefits of any attendant economic activity. To cite only two polluters, this would make motorists and pulp-mill operators liable for the air and water pollution they cause.

Implicit in such a course would be the problem of determining the true economic costs of the side effects of certain activities. For example, how is a price tag to be put on the destruction caused by pollution from a steel mill's smokestacks? In principle, a price can be figured out. But in practice, the task is far from simple and the difficulty is compounded by the problem of effectively assessing the cost against the actual polluter.

Assessing the costs in the case of oil spills is complicated by the fact that the ocean (and frequently even the beaches) is not private property. They are a *common-property resource*, which means that no one owns them, and that everyone can use them. If somebody did own them, that person would do what any other property owner does when suffering damage: sue the polluter for the full extent of the damages. This points to one direction that public policy can take.

Lawmakers, however, do not usually think in terms of property rights, but rather in terms of required safety devices or outright prohibitions. Faced with the imminent arrival of oil from Alaska, the state of Washington has been grappling with ways to reduce the likelihood of oil spills in Puget Sound. It passed a "tanker" law in 1975 which required that tankers of more than 50,000 dead-weight tons would have to use a pilot in the waters of Puget Sound. Further, the law barred tankers of more than 125,000 dead-weight tons from entering the sound and

---

[3] It is easy for people to assert that *all* pollution should be stopped; but the economy will have less real income if the costs of total elimination of pollution exceed the benefits.

prohibited any tanker of between 40,000 and 125,000 dead-weight tons from entering the sound unless it was escorted by tugs or equipped with twin screws, collision-avoidance radar, and a double bottom. Atlantic Richfield Company challenged the law. A three-judge panel did, in fact, strike it down. Their decision will probably be taken to the U.S. Supreme Court. The issue is still undecided. One proposal is to require that all tankers be double-hulled. Still another alternative has been to establish a traffic control system analogous to the system that now controls commercial aircraft movements. Plans are also under way to establish a tanker port in the straits of Juan de Fuca outside Puget Sound and then have a pipeline connect with oil refiners in the sound. The establishment of such a tanker port would be coupled with either an outright prohibition of large tankers in the sound or a prohibitive tax (say, $10 a barrel) for tanker movements in the sound. Are these policies preferable to making the polluter liable? In part, the answer depends on whether the **liability** is limited or unlimited.

If liability is limited, then the small tank barge may be discouraged from operating, while the owners of the 300,000-ton tanker will take their chances. Here's why. Suppose liability for oil spills could not exceed $100,000. If a small 50,000-ton independent tanker spilled its load, it could mean financial ruin or at least crippling losses for the company. But if a 300,000-ton super tanker from Atlantic Richfield were to break apart, the maximum liability assessment would be a far lighter penalty relative to the potential profits from that superload of oil. Under any given profitability of foundering, the supertanker will sail because potential profits are large enough to warrant risking a spillage fine. The small, one-ship company has no such comfortable assurance. Therefore, in order for the laws to be effective against oil spills, they must contain unlimited-liability clauses.

What would be the result of such laws? Oil carriers would be forced to carry insurance sufficient to cover damages. The high costs of such coverage would probably eliminate giant tankers from some enclosed waters such as Puget Sound or Chesapeake Bay, where the potential liability from a major oil spill would be of immense magnitude. Insurance premiums would decline with improvements in safety devices designed to prevent accidental oil spillage. Operators would therefore be encouraged to install such measures. There would also be an incentive to improve the technology of cleaning up oil spills and thereby to reduce the costs of damages. The suggested program would undoubtedly raise the price of petroleum products to consumers, since all of these alternatives would increase costs.

Such state, national, and international legislation would not solve all the problems connected with oil spills. As in the cases of narcotics and crime (Chapters 2 and 20), one challenge must always be the detection and identification of the culprit. A "finder's fee" for reporting polluters might provide some assistance. The above suggestions point toward a solution common to many ecological dilemmas—property rights will have to be realigned if private and social costs (and benefits) are to coincide. As long as individuals, firms, or even governmental units can foist some of the costs of their actions onto others, they will be human enough to do so. But if reorganized property rights can force polluters to bear the full costs of their actions, they will have every incentive to act responsibly.

SUMMARY

Most oceans are common property. Therefore, the problem of oil spills typically must be solved by governments that claim territorial sovereignty over many of the waters in the world. It would be simple if governments could make the perpetrators of oil spills pay the value of the damages caused. Several problems arise with such a system, however. First, it is often difficult to detect the perpetrator of oil spills, particularly if they occur in open waters. Second, it is not easy to determine the value of the economic damages caused. Third, it is not often easy to pay each individual who has been harmed by the oil spill. And fourth, the value of the economic damages sustained due to an oil spill may exceed the **net worth** of the company responsible for the oil spill. Nonetheless, one option is to require unlimited liability insurance on the part of tanker owners. The costs of insurance will, of course, be passed on to the consumer in the form of higher prices for oil products.

DISCUSSION QUESTIONS

1. What is the difference between limited and unlimited liability and how would this difference affect the number of oil spills that occur in the United States?
2. What ways are there to encourage better technology for the clean-up of oil spills? Are these ways similar to those that would encourage a reduction in the number of oil spills?

23

the economics of
Flooding Hell's Canyon

Hell's Canyon, on the Snake River separating Oregon from Idaho, is the deepest canyon on the North American continent, exceeding even the Grand Canyon. It offers some of the most spectacular scenery in the country; it is a natural habitat for elk, deer, and bighorn sheep; the hillsides echo to the call of vast flocks of redleg partridge; and the rushing river contains salmon, steelhead, and sturgeon.

Hell's Canyon is also perhaps the best remaining site in the United States for developing hydroelectric power. The results of such a development would be a high dam that would turn the river into a huge lake, backing it all the way up to an already existing dam and lake farther up the river.

Should this new dam be built?

The issue created a controversy that has continued for many years. During this time the plans and proposed sites for the dam have changed. The protagonists on either side have also changed (in some cases they have even changed sides). And what was once a controversy between public and private power over two alternative and mutually exclusive dam sites has become a debate between those who want no dam at all and the unified forces of the public and private power groups who contended that the dam should be constructed and operated by their joint efforts.

While rhetoric and power politics dominated the headlines, the issue was fought before the Federal Power Commission with numbers. The numbers were plugged into cost-benefit analyses of the dam; and, since several alternative dam combinations were proposed, alternative cost-benefit analyses were developed. We shall look at just one—the High Mountain Sheep Dam, clearly the most impressive hydroelectric proposal.

Cost-benefit analysis has been developed to help determine the **social costs** as distinguished from the **private costs** of economic activities. What's the difference? For the production of a vast array of goods and services there is either no difference, or one so small that no one bothers about it. In such cases, the private opportunity costs of the amount of capital and the expected returns dictate whether to undertake an economic activity. For instance, if a predicted rate of return exceeds the opportunity cost of capital for a proposed factory, the factory will be built.

However, where externalities exist—that is, where benefits or costs accrue to persons other than the investor (and the user)—the purely private calculation may yield the wrong decision from the viewpoint of society as a whole. In the case of the High Mountain Sheep Dam project, a private investor undertaking the project would not get the benefits of the additional power that could be generated at downstream power plants as a result of regulating the flow of the river and releasing more water at periods of low stream flow. Nor would a private investor reap the benefits from reducing flood damage in the lower Snake and Columbia rivers as a result of reducing stream flow in periods of high water and potential flooding. On the other hand, neither would that investor bear the cost to society of destroying or damaging the runs of migratory fish; reducing wildlife habitats of both waterfowl and mammals; and irrevocably altering the scenic beauty of a unique and irreplaceable area.

Some of these externalities are relatively easy to measure. One is the downstream benefits of a dam, which are simply the value of the additional power generated times the price per kilowatt-hour. Another is the value of reduced flood damage, which can be calculated by assessing how much damage might be done downstream by the amount of water to be stored, and multiplying that figure by the frequency with which such high water would occur in the absence of the dam (this data being obtainable from historical river records). But who can measure the externalities involved in the destruction of the aesthetic grandeur and recreational value of a previously undeveloped canyon? Let's see how this calculation was attempted in the case of High Mountain Sheep Dam.

Omitting, for the moment, the external costs associated with altering the environment, opponents of the dam measured all other costs and benefits of the proposed dam versus the next-best alternative, which was nuclear power. They then asked what value would have to be placed on preservation of the original environment to justify *not* building the dam.[1] The conclusion was that over its projected 50-year life span, the High Mountain Sheep Dam would provide benefits over its next-best alternative of between $14 and $24 million, depending on assumptions made about other dams and the nuclear alternative.

A brief resumé of the way the figures were derived will illustrate the usual procedure in such cases. The total investment cost of the dam, at an interest rate of 9 percent, was calculated at $266,786,000. Bonds would be floated at that interest rate to provide that sum. This brought the total annual costs (fixed charges on the bonds, plus costs for operating, generating, and transmission) to $39,597,000.

On the benefit side, the power benefits (presumably including downstream benefits) were $41,894,000 annually and the

[1] The following data are drawn from Dr. John Krutilla's testimony before the Federal Power Commission.

flood-control benefits were $245,000 annually, for a total of $42,139,000. Gross annual costs subtracted from gross annual benefits thus leave a net benefit of $2,542,000 annually. This comes to $24,068,000 over the 50-year life span of the project.

The last figure should bother you: a net annual benefit of $2.5 million multiplied by 50 years comes to a lot more than $24 million. But in fact it does not, because a dollar earned today is considerably more valuable than a dollar earned next year, and about 75 times as valuable as a dollar earned 50 years hence. The reason for this is quite simple. We must ask how many of today's dollars will be needed to make $2.5 million next year, recognizing that today's dollars can earn perhaps 9 percent (that is, their opportunity costs and the rate at which we **discount** future dollars). A few simple calculations will convince you that the present value of $2.5 million 50 years from now (that is, the number of today's dollars needed to provide $2.5 million at 9 percent annual compound interest) is not that great. So the further away the benefit in time and the higher the opportunity cost of money (the interest rate), the lower the present value. The same reasoning applies to costs. When all the arithmetic is worked out, $24 million appears as the upper-bound estimate. The lower-bound estimate of $14 million was calculated in similar fashion using a different interest (discount) rate.

Now we come to the critical question. Is the value of preserving the existing canyon equal to $14–$24 million over the next 50 years? How do you measure the enjoyment of a natural scenic attraction? The ideal answer would be obtained by assessing what people would be willing to pay to maintain the canyon. We have no answer, but we can get a general idea by making some comparisons. We find that in Norway, for example, where streams can be owned privately, sports fishermen are willing to pay as much as $500 a day for fishing rights in certain Atlantic salmon stream areas. Since the steelhead is a close cousin of the Atlantic salmon, this figure gives us some notion of the value people place upon such fishing in Hell's Canyon. Canadian Atlantic salmon leasing prices give further information. We could also investigate how willing people have been to pay for hunting and other forms of recreation under market conditions by making similar comparisons.

Furthermore, it is clear that the value of recreational resources is growing each year, as increased income and leisure time enable more and more people to enjoy such facilities. Since the demand is increasing at all prices but the supply is fixed,[2] the value will inevitably keep rising. Overall, by such approximations, the authors of the rebuttal study for High Mountain Sheep Dam concluded that the recreational benefits of the original canyon do indeed surpass the $14–$24 million of benefits to be expected from hydroelectric development.

When we wrote the first edition of this book, the issue was still in doubt. Now it is settled. Was it resolved by cold cost-benefit calculus? Hardly! While the figures undoubtedly had some influence, the final determination was made in the political arena by Congress, which passed a law prohibiting further dam construction on that portion of the Snake River.

SUMMARY

To assess the costs and benefits of a proposed project, one must look to the future. Future costs and benefits must be discounted back to the present in order to find the net present value of the proposed project. Only if the net present value of the proposed project is positive can we consider it to be a potentially useful one. Of course, our cost-benefit analysis will always be incomplete, owing to the lack of good information about the potential costs and potential benefits of a change in our environment.

DISCUSSION QUESTIONS

1. Why is a dollar in costs a year from now worth less than a dollar in costs today? Why is a dollar in benefits to be received a year from now worth less than a dollar in benefits received today?
2. List some potential costs of constructing a dam on the Snake River. Do you think these costs are all easily quantifiable?

[2] Theoretically, substitutes do exist, but it is not clear how close they really are.

24

the economics of
Clamming and Other "Free" Goods

The razor clam (*Siliqua patula*) is a large bivalve of the Solenidae family that inhabits the ocean beaches of the Pacific Coast, from California to Alaska. Once a major staple of the coastal Indian population, it is now a major prey of the white man escaping the city for the ocean beaches. (Cleaned, cut into steaks, dipped in batter, fried one minute on each side, and served with a bottle of dry white wine, it is superb).

These clams are dug in minus tides, and the beach area they inhabit is not, at least in the state of Washington, private property. Therefore, access is available to everyone, and the only costs of digging clams are cut fingers and an occasional dunking in icy water. Nobody owns them; they are a common-property resource, a **free good**. But this fact does not make clams any less subject to economic analysis than goods with price tags on them. A **demand schedule** exists for clamming. Like other demand schedules, it shows that more people will use more of the product at a low price than at a high one; and that how *much* more they use will depend on **elasticity of demand** (that is, degree of responsiveness to a given change in price). When the price is zero, as it was in clamming until the summer of 1979, the amount used will certainly be much more than at any level of positive price. Again, how much more depends on the elasticity of the demand schedule.

We can also derive, hypothetically at least, a supply curve, although to discover positive prices we would have to envision private ownership of beaches and see how many clams would be offered by beach owners at various prices. The higher the price, the more would be offered. Presumably, if the price were right, the owner would incur costs of "cultivating" and protecting clam beds to increase their yield.

If a market situation existed, an equilibrium price and quantity could be established; but since a wide gap is inevitable between the amount demanded at zero price and the amount supplied at zero price, some device must ration the product. State authorities take on this task by setting daily catch limits and closing certain seasons to clamming. Regulations for the state of Washington first allowed noncommercial diggers to take 15 clams a day on any ocean beach from midnight to noon between March 16 and June 30. Unfortunately, these regulations were only a short-run solution. In the distant past, when the Pacific Coast was sparsely settled, no particular problem existed (in fact, no limit or season was set, since in those days, even at a zero price, the supply exceeded the demand).[1] But each year more and more people have more income for traveling to beaches and more leisure to devote to clamming. The result is that the demand keeps increasing, and each year happy clam hunters crowd the minus-tide beaches. In Oregon, the clam-seeking camper sometimes faces lines as much as a mile long.

[1] By 1925, regulations did limit commercial harvesting of Washington razor clams to the months of March, April, and May. A well-trained clam digger can remove as much as half a ton of clams during one low tide. There was no need then to restrict the season for noncommercial clam digging.

The supply also may increase if new beaches are opened up or if the State Fisheries Department attempts to cultivate more clams on existing beaches. But the increase can be only minimal once all the beaches have been made accessible. The ultimate result must inevitably be more crowding and fewer clams each year. It is not a happy prospect.

The clamming story is repeated over and over again for recreational activities, and the same analysis applies. In the case of wilderness areas, the supply is actually decreasing rather than merely remaining constant. All over the country, fishing, hunting, and camping sites are overcrowded, although these areas have somewhat greater potential for expansion of supply.

What is being done to improve the situation? A price is charged for fishing and hunting in the form of license fees, and more recently camping sites in parks are being "rented." In 1979, the Washington state legislature finally established a $2.50 resident (and $10 nonresident) clamming license. In each case, however, the rates have been set so far below the equilibrium price, which could balance quantities supplied with quantities demanded, that they are not even close to resolving the problem of overcrowding. And each year it gets worse. Anyone wishing to test the proposition need only visit Yellowstone or Yosemite National Park in the summer.

Contrast the case of clams with that of the oyster beds in the state of Washington, which were privately owned before the state restricted private ownership of tidal land. Those oyster beds were treated as an asset in which investment was made to improve the yield. In fact, the oysters are farmed just like any other agricultural commodity. Perhaps a more spectacular contrast is between the north and south shores of Chesapeake Bay. On the north shore, the state of Maryland has made the oyster beds a common-property resource; and, as would be expected where entry was unlimited, severe depletion has occurred. Moreover, it has not been worthwhile to privately invest in improving the yield. In order to cut down on the harvest, the state has forced the use of archaic harvesting tools and archaic propulsion requirements (that is, oyster dredging can only be done under sail power). In contrast, the state of Virginia on the south shore of the bay allows private ownership of tidal lands. With 80 percent of the tidal land in private hands, owners have developed the oyster beds into a thriving sustained enterprise. The average output per worker was 59 percent higher in Virginia than in Maryland during the 25-year period 1945–1969.[2]

Why are we content with a zero, or now a nominal, price for clamming or for fishing? The answer is that the American people have long believed that such activities are a hereditary right, that they should be equally accessible to rich and poor alike, and that charging a fee favors the rich (which it certainly does). This argument prevails in the cases of clamming, fishing, and hunting, but not in the case of buying yachts and airplanes. The result is to artificially lower the price for a particular publicly owned commodity—clams—but not for all commodities. In effect, the public policy is saying that income should not be a factor in people's ability to clam or to fish, but that it can be in buying golf clubs, TV sets, or airplanes. In effect, this is a policy of selective income redistribution.

As crowding, rationing, and queuing become more and more severe in such nonpriced or underpriced activities, it becomes a major issue to determine whether rationing by price or by quantity restriction is the better method. One alternative is to eliminate the common-property aspects of such resources. Another is for the government to set a price that approximates a market price. The final alternative consists of a variety of rationing devices to restrict quantity more and more rigidly.

SUMMARY

Some have called common-property resources "free" goods. Actually, the fact that a resource is common property does not mean it is free. It may only be free in the sense that the explicit monetary

[2] Richard J. Agnello and Lawrence P. Donnelley, "Property Rights and Efficiency in the Oyster Industry," *Journal of Law and Economics*, vol. 18, no. 2 (October 1975), p. 531.

price that is paid is zero. The cost to society is, of course, always going to be greater than zero, provided that the quantity supplied at a zero price is less than the quantity demanded. Because an excess quantity is demanded at a zero price, the state imposes regulations to prevent the overconsumption of "free" goods such as clams. Also, user fees have been imposed, but they are typically well below a price that would equate quantity demanded with quantity supplied.

DISCUSSION QUESTIONS

1. Clams are not really "free" goods, but rather goods sold at a low or zero price. Are there, in fact, any truly free goods in our society?
2. In the case of oysters, there seems to be no problem of overconsumption. What is the difference between the farming of clams and oysters?

25

the economics of
Auto Congestion

When you drive on a highway at rush hour, or on a major street in a big city, you find yourself either driving slowly or standing still. There used to be a saying in Los Angeles that each newly built freeway was obsolete the day it opened. Why? Because of automobile congestion. In virtually every city in America, the problem of auto congestion at rush hour is a serious one. The proffered solution is typically to build more highways, byways, freeways, expressways, bridges, and the like.

What is the cause of this supposed overuse of roadways? The answer is not hard to find. For the most part, individuals who drive at rush hour are not explicitly charged a higher money price to use the resource called a roadway at that particular time. However, users of many other resources *are* charged a higher price during peak periods. Alternatively, they can use the resource at off-peak periods at a lower price. For example, many movie theaters have a sliding-scale price schedule that starts at a lower figure before, say, 2:00 P.M., jumps to a higher figure between 2:00 and 6:00 P.M., and is at its highest level after 6:00 P.M. Seats for broadway plays, concerts, and the like, usually cost more on weekends than they do during the week or at a matinee. Many restaurants offer so-called early bird specials between 5:00 and 7:00 P.M., when food and drinks cost less than they would later in the evening.

But for roadway usage, such is usually not the case. If you decide to drive to work at 8:00 A.M., you pay the same nominal price you would pay if you left at 6:30 A.M. That nominal monetary price is zero. But, of course, congestion does impose a cost on society; the cost is the increased time it takes everyone to travel during periods of congestion. (The input—the size of the roadway—is typically fixed, although for some bridges and roadways, a middle lane can be made reversible depending on the flow of traffic.) In other words, travelers suffer increased marginal costs when going to and from their destinations at peak periods (other costs, such as road maintenance, may increase also, but we will not deal with them here).

Several years ago, a study was undertaken to compare marginal costs, expressed in cents-per-vehicle mile, during peak periods with costs during near-peak and off-peak periods. The study focused on the San Francisco expressway system, and the cost was measured in terms of one more vehicle mile added to the expressway. At peak periods, the marginal cost in cents-per-vehicle mile was shown to be 38.1 cents; at near-peak periods, 8.9 cents; and at off-peak periods, 7.7 cents.[1] Clearly, the marginal costs created by auto congestion are substantial.

If this is generally so, wouldn't one solution to the problem be to charge users higher prices for peak-period use of the roadway resources? The answer is certainly yes. However, a problem arises in finding a practical way to impose peak-period pricing

[1] T. E. Keeler and K. A. Small, "Optimal Peak-Load Pricing, Investment, and Service Levels on Urban Expressways," *Journal of Political Economy*, vol. 85, no. 1 (February 1944), pp. 1–26, table 5.

for automobiles. In the case of bridges where a toll is already collected, it would be relatively simple because the mechanism is mostly in place. The bridge authority need only raise the price to those who use the bridge during peak morning and evening periods or, alternatively, lower the price to those using the bridge at off-peak periods. In most locales, just the opposite approach is used—that is, a reverse peak-load pricing is in effect in the form of commuter passes. Typically, a booklet of passes for crossing a toll bridge is sold in which the per-unit price is lower than if each crossing were paid for individually. Since the purchasers of commuter booklets are usually those who use the bridge at peak periods, this system actually encourages individuals to use the bridge during peak periods.

Freeways, expressways, and the like present a more difficult problem. Because a majority of these roadways are not toll roads, a new toll system would have to be evolved and there would certainly be congestion at the toll booths. Currently, highway usage is paid for indirectly through a system of surcharges on gasoline purchases. Gasoline purchases are about proportional to mileage traveled, so in essence everyone pays a uniform charge per mile for all highway usage. The commute to the office on the congested freeway is priced at about the same figure per mile as the Sunday drive in the country.

Any system that tried to impose peak-load pricing surcharges for highway usage would be bound to raise a few hackles. The argument will always be made that only the well-to-do would benefit because only they could afford access to the uncongested highways during peak periods. Of course, this argument ignores the possibility of car pooling and the alternative use of mass transit. But, the major barrier is one of implementation. As a result, most countries have made little effort to implement any congestion-pricing system.

One tiny city-state has, however, been running an experiment. Singapore is an island republic of 2.3 million people pressed into 225 square miles. With over a quarter of a million private automobiles in existence, rush hour in that city is something to be seen. In the mid-seventies, Singapore adopted a system of area licensing, a system designed to increase the price of roadways in congested areas of the city during peak periods. Private automobiles must now exhibit a special license to enter the controlled area. Each area is approximately a quarter of a mile on each side of the controlled area. The peak period lasts from 7:30 A.M. to 10:15 A.M. The license costs approximately $30 per month and can also be purchased on a daily basis.

Enforcement is, of course, a problem, but it seems to be a manageable one, and is indeed handled very well by a small traffic police force stationed at the entry points of the controlled areas. To ease the burden for individuals who felt unable to pay the $30 per month, the government provided additional bus-transit service, as well as additional parking facilities for transit users outside the downtown area. Additionally, four-person car pools were exempted from the license fee.

The results? Quite a success, for congestion has been reduced significantly. After implementation of the plan, the total volume of traffic fell almost 50 percent during the restricted hours. The marginal cost of commuting in terms of time has fallen dramatically, both for those who drive and for those who use an alternative mode of transportation.

SUMMARY

Auto congestion imposes high marginal costs on those who choose to drive at peak hours. Auto congestion continues to occur because the resource called roadways is not priced differentially to meet the change in demand between peak and off-peak periods. One solution would be for toll bridges and roads to impose a peak period surcharge to reduce the quantity of use demanded during peak periods. The centers of many cities would reduce auto congestion by following the lead of Singapore, which has established an area licensing system requiring a special license to enter the controlled downtown area. Increasing the explicit monetary marginal cost to drivers reduces the quantity demanded of peak-period central-core driving.

DISCUSSION QUESTIONS

1. Every time an argument is raised in favor of using the price system to allocate a scarce resource, the issue of "the poor not being able to afford it" arises. Is this a valid issue?

2. When you enter a roadway at a peak period, what is the marginal cost of your action? Can you think of a practical way to measure the marginal cost of your action? (Hint: What is the marginal cost sustained by the average driver using the same roadway?)

26

the economics of
Taxis and Jitneys

The fact that you probably never heard the word "jitney" says something about the problems we wish to pose in this chapter. Jitneys, to all intents and purposes, disappeared from the urban American scene some time ago. But jitneys and taxis have formed a major basis of the transportation in urban areas at various times. For our purposes they illustrate a major dilemma on the transportation scene: namely, the use of political policies and regulatory devices in municipalities to restrict or eliminate certain kinds of competition, with consequences for the overall efficiency of transportation in America.

The dictionary defines a jitney as a "bus or car, especially one traveling a regular route, that carries passengers for a small fare, originally five cents." Believe it or not, there are a few places in the United States where jitneys still exist, such as along Chicago's King Drive, San Francisco's Mission Street, and Atlantic

City's Pacific Avenue. The jitney, however, is a common form of transportation in many foreign cities, such as in Mexico City, along the Paseo de la Reforma, where it is called a *pesero*. The principle of a jitney is simple. A vehicle, usually a normal-sized sedan but sometimes a small minibus, travels along a usually fixed route, picking up customers anywhere along that route until the vehicle is filled and dropping those customers off wherever they designate along that fixed route. In a modified situation, the jitney will (for an additional fee, of course) take a customer off the route but within a limited range, only to return to the point of deviation for continuance along the same route. The difference between a jitney and a regular taxi is that the latter cannot generally pick up more than one paying set of customers at a time and does not follow a fixed route. (As we shall see, these restrictions are usually imposed by law, not by the taxi drivers.)

Jitneys appeared on the American transportation scene prior to our entry into World War I. When they first appeared, they offered advantages over the then-prevalent mode of public transportation—electric street railways—the chief one being a higher average speed. That speed of 15 miles an hour was still twice as fast as streetcar speeds. Jitneys were also allowed greater flexibility in their routes as compared with the absolutely fixed route of street railways.

The advantages of jitneys were sufficient at the prices charged for them to pose a serious competitive threat to electric railway systems throughout the United States. In fact the *Electric Railway Journal* started calling jitneys "a menace," the "Frankenstein of transportation," and various other epithets. A competing mode of transportation threatened to erode the profits of railway systems in municipalities. A general rule of thumb is: If when faced with competition you cannot compete on an economic basis, try the political arena. That is exactly what the railways did: they sought protection from the governments of the municipalities in which they were located. In spite of scattered newspaper support for projitney political policies, the efforts of jitney association lobbyists, and the obviously anticompetitive implications of antijitney legislation, restrictive legislation was passed throughout the United States.

At first the legislation required jitney operators to obtain licenses to use public streets as a place of business. This restriction drastically reduced the ease of entering the business, particularly since the municipalities made it lengthy and costly to obtain the permit or license. In some cities a license or franchise had to be submitted to voters! Additional costs were imposed, such as the requirement that relatively large liability bonds be purchased to protect the consumer of jitney services should a wrong be committed against him by a jitney operator. In some cases, the cost of licensing fees plus bonding requirements equaled 50 percent of a jitney driver's annual earnings. This is the equivalent of a tax in that amount on drivers. In a highly competitive industry, in which the individual participants were not making excessive profits, such a tax could only lead to one result—the elimination of a significant fraction of the industry's participants.

Further restrictions were added that basically eliminated the jitney as a form of public transportation in the United States. These included a requirement that any jitney had to be operated a minimum number of hours, that minimum usually exceeding the average number of hours that jitneys were usually run; the fixing of routes and schedules, which eliminated the flexibility that jitneys offered; and the exclusion of jitneys from high-density downtown areas and specifically from trolley routes—the most advantageous working locations for the jitney drivers.[1] According to L. R. Nash,[2] a student of jitney history, within 18 months of the appearance of jitneys in Los Angeles, antijitney (i.e., protrolley) regulatory ordinances had been passed in 125 of the 175

[1] In 1974 the Los Angeles City Council removed its prohibition on jitney service. However, a proposed ordinance was soon put forth allowing the municipal bus system to restrict jitneys from operating along major bus routes. The city bus system successfully quashed plans to allow jitneys along heavily traveled routes. (History repeats itself.)

[2] L. R. Nash, "History and Economics of the Jitney," Stone and Webster Journal, vol. 18 (1916), pp. 361, 365.

cities in which jitneys competed with trolleys. Most major municipalities acted similarly within another year.

The elimination of the jitney industry certainly benefited the electric trolleys, but it also benefited the taxi industry, which we present as another example of restricted competition.

In most cities in the United States, not just anyone can legally drive a taxi, and those who drive one legally are restricted in many ways. Most importantly, they are restricted to specific geographic areas and in the price they charge a customer. That price is generally regulated by a commission and is uniform at all times of day for all taxis.

In the taxi business in many cities, the potential owner-operator of a cab must purchase what is called a medallion. The ownership of this medallion gives the owner the legal right to operate a taxi within a specified area. So far so good. However, for example, in New York City the price of these medallions has at times gone up to $30,000 and the price has reached similarly astronomical heights in other cities. How, you might ask, could the right to operate a taxicab cost so much? Clearly, the medallion is inexpensive to produce, even if it is made out of bronze.

The key to understanding this issue is understanding that there is generally a *fixed* number of medallions available. In other words, entry into the taxicab business in many cities in the United States is limited by law to zero. That is the only reason a medallion owner can sell his or her rights to the taxicab operation to another person for such a high figure. The person buying the medallion would not pay such a price unless he or she was fairly certain that no new competition would exist in the future, and that present monopoly rates of return, or profits, would continue into the indefinite future for any owner of a medallion. Naturally, those monopoly profits can only exist so long as the monopoly exists, and in a situation in which potential entry merely involves putting a sign on a four-door sedan reading "Taxi for Hire," the possibility of competition—eliminating any monopoly profits—is great. Only legislation designed for preventing entry can effectively ward off competition—that is, the police power of the state must be used to protect the monopoly position of individuals in the taxicab business. The documentation on the legislation perpetuating monopolies in cities such as Los Angeles, Dallas, Fort Worth, Philadelphia, Cleveland, New York, and Chicago is impressive, undeniably illustrating a classic case of restricted entry.

As you might expect, if the number of taxicabs is too severely limited, the potential for cheaters or interlopers in the existing monopoly situation is great. In fact, the "problem" of illegal or "gypsy" cabs operating in New York City is well known. Apparently officials turn a more or less deaf ear to this problem, recognizing that the limitation on the number of medallions has become too severe given the growing population of the city. The same is true in Chicago, where the gypsies are occasionally picked up but only fined $100. In general, there seems to be more toleration of illegal taxicabs in ghetto areas in New York, St. Louis, Pittsburgh, and perhaps Chicago. In such areas, there is a demand for taxis because of the diffuse home-work situations. Moreover, there is a relatively large supply of illegal taxicabs and taxicab operators because of the large number of unemployed individuals living in those sections who know how to drive.

It has been suggested that a way to solve urban transportation problems would be to lift the restrictions against jitneys, and against the proliferation of taxis, by removing legislation prohibiting individuals from going into business for themselves. Note, however, that if this were done, all current owners of taxi licenses would suffer windfall losses. After all, those who benefited from restriction on entry into the business were the *original* owners of the licenses or the monopoly rights. The current owners had to pay a competitive price to obtain those rights, and that price included all future monopoly profits that the original owners perceived would exist. Current owners only make a normal rate of return, and they would suffer losses if the valuable asset—the medallion—that they purchased at a price of, say, $25,000 became worth zero.

Another possibility is to lift all restrictions on taxicab and jitney operations in certain cities while compensating current owners of monopoly rights for their windfall losses. If this were to occur, the urban transportation mess might be ameliorated, though it certainly would not be solved.

SUMMARY

Jitneys were put out of business in the United States through the political activities of municipal railway systems. Today, an additional political force preventing their reemergence in most cities is the taxicab monopoly. In many major cities, taxi ownership interests have succeeded in establishing a monopoly market structure in which only those who have a medallion (license) can legally operate a taxicab or a fleet of taxicabs. The value of the medallion on the open market is equivalent to the (discounted) profits over and above the competitive rate of return. In New York City, it has at times had a value as high as $30,000. Open competition in the taxicab market, or effective competition by illegal gypsy cabs, would reduce the value of the medallion severely. In the extreme case, it would have a zero value.

DISCUSSION QUESTIONS

1. What are some of the justifications for taxicab licensing?
2. What would happen to the market value of medallions if jitneys were allowed?

27

the economics of
Selling
Pollution Rights

Pollution, almost by definition, is undesirable. There are numerous ways to reduce or avoid pollution. Laws can be passed banning production processes that emit pollutants into the air and water, or specifying a minimum air quality level or the maximum amount of pollution allowable. Firms would then be responsible for developing the technology and for paying the price to satisfy such standards. Or, the law could specify the particular type of production technology to be used, and the type of pollution-abatement equipment required in order to legally produce. Finally, subsidies could be paid to firms that reduce pollution emission, or taxes could be imposed on firms that engage in pollution emission.

No matter which methods are used to reduce pollution, problems will arise. For example, setting physical limits on the amount of pollution permitted would discourage firms from developing the technology that would limit pollution beyond those limits. The alternative of subsidizing firms that reduce pollution levels may seem a strange use of taxpayers' dollars. The latest "solution" to the air pollution problem—selling the rights to pollute—may seem even stranger. Nonetheless, this approach is now being used in the majority of states. Men like Stewart Rupp of Richmond, California, a partner in an environmental consulting firm, work as brokers, helping companies trade the right to pollute.

To understand how this situation came about, we must understand the Federal Clean Air Act. This act was passed in 1963 in an attempt to force a reduction in pollution, particularly in metropolitan areas in the United States. Through rules and regulations of the EPA, the Clean Air Act presents localities with specified permitted pollution levels. These so-called National Air Quality Standards must be met in most major metropolitan areas. However, in many of these areas air quality is already poor. Thus, a company that wishes to build a plant in such an area is theoretically barred from doing so because of its detrimental impact on air quality. If the guidelines were strictly adhered to, it would mean no further industrial growth in many urban areas.

The Environmental Protection Agency approved an offset policy to get around this problem. A company that wants to build a new plant is required to work out a corresponding reduction in pollution at some existing plant. For example, when Volkswagen wanted to build a plant in New Stanton, Pennsylvania, the state of Pennsylvania agreed to reduce pollutants from its highway-paving operations. This reduction would offset the Volkswagen plant's pollution.

One major problem with the offset policy involves the difficulty in finding an offset partner. In other words, each time a firm wants to build a new plant in an already polluted area, it must seek, on an individual basis, an offset partner that agrees to reduce pollution (usually after a payment from the other company). This is where the idea of brokering the right to pollute comes into play. This is where people like Stewart Rupp can go to work.

A company that closes a plant or installs improved pollution-abatement equipment can receive "emission credits" for its clean-up efforts, credits that can be purchased by another firm. The industry negotiates the price. For example, the Times Mirror Company was able to complete a $120 million expansion of a paper-making plant near Portland, Oregon, after it purchased emission credits allowing it to add 150 tons of extra hydrocarbons into the atmosphere each year. A woodcoating plant and a dry-cleaning firm had gone out of business; they sold the necessary credits for $50,000 to the Times Mirror.

Using a broker to find firms that have emission credits to sell does not solve all the problems with the offset policy. Wisconsin is setting up a computer system to track available credits for a nationwide trading system. In Illinois, the chamber of commerce and state environmental office established a clearinghouse to handle a market for the trading of pollution rights. More such centralized marketplaces are sure to spring up, since about 45 states have already adopted regulations or issued permits allowing some form of air pollution offsets.

One of the benefits of a pollution rights "bank," as it were, is the increased economic incentive to reduce pollution levels below those required by law. A firm that believes it could cheaply reduce pollutants further would find out that at some point another firm would pay it for such a reduction in order to build a new plant. Presumably, such a marketplace for the right to pollute would encourage further research and development in pollution-reduction techniques. Today, many standards are set on an absolute physical basis, offering companies no additional incentive to reduce pollution below the air quality standard.

SUMMARY

A strict physical standard for the amount of air pollution allowable in the atmosphere in any given geographic area can prevent change and growth in a dynamic economy. After all, some firms go out of business and others want to go into business. If each firm has the right to a certain amount of pollution and if it can sell "emission credits," then this problem is surmounted. Under this system, firms that go out of business, firms that develop techniques to reduce pollution, or firms that cut back on production —thereby reducing pollution—can sell their emission credits to firms wanting to expand or to go into business in the same geographical area. Also, if the cost of increased pollution abatement is less than the market price for the emission credits, more pollution abatement will occur per unit of total output produced in the United States.

DISCUSSION QUESTIONS

1. Does marketing the right to pollute mean that we are allowing too much destruction of our environment?
2. Who implicitly has property rights in the air if a pollution bank is set up and the right to pollute is sold to the highest bidder?

the economics of
Crime
and
Punishment

Is there a relationship between punishment and the number and types of crimes committed? If so, what are the available alternatives to punishing guilty offenders? Should we impose large fines instead of incarceration? Should we have public whippings? Should capital punishment be allowed? To establish a system of crime deterrence, we would need to assess carefully the value of different supposed deterrents.

One thing we can be sure of. Uniformly heavy punishments for all crimes will lead to a larger number of major crimes being committed. Let's look at the reasoning. All decisions are made on the margin. If an act of theft will be punished by hanging and an act of murder will be punished by the same fate, there is no marginal deterrence to murder. If a theft of $5 is met with a punishment of ten years in jail and a theft of $50,000 incurs the same sentence, why not steal $50,000? Why not go for broke? There is no marginal deterrence to prevent one from doing so.

A serious question is how our system of justice can establish penalties that are appropriate from a social point of view. To establish the correct (marginal) deterrents, we must observe empirically how criminals respond to changes in punishments. This leads us to the question of how people decide whether to commit a "crime." A theory needs to be established as to what determines the supply of criminal offenses.

Adam Smith once said:

> The affluence of the rich excites the indignation of the poor, who are often both driven by want, and prompted by envy, to invade his possessions. It is only under the shelter of the civil magistrate that the owner of that valuable property, which is acquired by the labour of many years, or perhaps by many successive generations, can sleep a single night in security. He is at all times surrounded by unknown enemies, whom, though he never provokes, he can never appease, and from whose injustice he can be protected only by the powerful arm of the civil magistrate continually held up to chastise it. The acquisition of valuable and extensive property, therefore, necessarily requires the establishment of civil government. Where there is no property, or at least none that exceeds the value of two or three days' labour, civil government is not so necessary.[1]

Smith is pointing out that robberies involve the taking of valuable property. Thus, we can surmise that individuals who engage in robberies are seeking income. Therefore, before acting, a professional criminal might be expected to look at the anticipated returns and the anticipated costs of criminal activity. These could then be compared with the net returns from legitimate activities. We note that the civil government which Smith refers to above would be imposing the cost on the criminal, if apprehended. That cost would include, but not be limited to, apprehension, conviction, and jail. (The criminal's calculations are analogous to those made by a professional athlete when weighing the cost of possible serious injury.)

Viewing the supply of offenses thusly, we can come up with methods by which society can lower the net expected rate of re-

---

[1] Adam Smith, *The Wealth of Nations*, 1776.

turn for committing any illegal activity. That is, we can figure out how to reduce crime most effectively. We have talked about one particular aspect—the size of penalties. We also briefly mentioned another—the probability of detection for each offense. When either of these costs of crime goes up, the supply of offenses goes down; that is, less crime is committed.

Can this theory be applied to a decision, pro or con, on capital punishment? Sociologists, psychologists, and others have numerous theories correlating the number of murders committed to various psychological, sociological, and demographic variables. In general, they have stressed social and psychological factors as determinants of violent crime and have therefore felt that capital punishment would have no deterrent effect. Economists, on the other hand, have stressed a cost-benefit equation, which implies that capital punishment would deter violent crime.

We start with a commodity called the act of murder. If the act of murder is like any other commodity, the quantity "demanded" (by perpetrators, of course, not victims) will be negatively related to the relative price. But what is the price of murder? Ignoring all the sociological, psychological, or psychic costs of murder, we have to consider the cost to the murderer if he or she is caught. Thus, we have to consider the probability of being caught, and, after capture, the possible jail sentence or capital punishment that may be called for. But here again, we have to look at the probability of a particular jail sentence and the probability of going to the gas chamber, or the guillotine, or the four winds. Thus, it would do little good to observe the difference in murder rates between states that have capital punishment and states that do not. Instead, we must assess the probability of a convicted murderer going to the gas chamber in states that have capital punishment and compare it to what happens in states that do not. In fact, there are some states with capital punishment where, effectively, the probability of a convicted murderer going to the gas chamber is zero. We find, for example, that states with the death penalty for first-degree murder often change the charge to second-degree murder. But states with life maximums for first-degree murder give those sentences more frequently.

Now, immediately, critics of such analysis point to the "fact" that the murderer, either in a moment of unreasoned passion or when confronted with an unanticipated situation, for example, during an armed robbery, does not take into account the expected probability of going to the gas chamber. That is to say, murderers are not acting rationally when they murder. Is this a valid criticism of the economic model of the demand for murder? It is not. If the **model** predicts poorly, then either the assumptions or the model must be changed. Indeed, if one contends that the expected "price" of committing a murder has no effect on the quantity of murders, one is implicitly negating the law of demand or stating that the price elasticity of the demand for murder is zero. One is also confusing the average murderer with the marginal murderer. All potential murderers do not have to be aware of or react to the change in the expected "price" of committing a murder for the theory to be useful. If a sufficient number of marginal murderers act as if they were responding to the higher expected "price" of murdering, then the demand curve for murders by perpetrators will be downward sloping.

A few economists have actually worked through economic models of the demand for murder and other crimes. One of the variables they included was the objective conditional risk of execution—in other words, the risk of being executed if caught and convicted of murder. Two elasticities given in one study were − 0.06 and − 0.065.[2] While these elasticities are relatively small, they are not zero. The implication of these elasticities, given the number of murders and executions in the period covered by the study (1935 to 1969) was striking. The implied tradeoff between murders and executions was between 7 and 8. "Put differently, an additional execution per year over the period in question may have resulted, on average, in 7 or 8 fewer murders."[3]

As might be expected, these findings are highly controversial and have led to a debate that still goes on. Critics have

[2] Isaac Erlich, "The Deterrent Effect of Capital Punishment: A Question of Life and Death," *The American Economic Review*, vol. 65, no. 3 (June 1973), p. 414.
[3] Ibid., p. 414.

stressed the tenuous statistical basis of the findings.[4] However, while the argument over capital punishment continues, the evidence that crime rates in general appear to vary inversely with estimates of penalties, probabilities of conviction, and legal opportunities, has received substantial support.[5]

One final note. In the case of capital punishment, the execution must be thought to fall on the guilty parties, rather than randomly applied. History tells us that under the emperors in China, executions were frequent. However, the emperors were not always so diligent about executing the right person. This system of "punishment" does little good for society in terms of combating crime, not to mention the loss suffered by the innocent victim and his or her family due to perverted justice.

SUMMARY

One can analyze criminal acts as economic activities. The potential criminal makes an economic decision in which he or she does a cost-benefit analysis of criminal activities versus legal consequences. A key set of variables in such an analysis involves the costs of criminal activity, which include the costs of getting caught, being sentenced, and suffering punishment. In most major cities, the probabilities of being caught, sentenced, going to trial, and serving time are very low. Hence, when they are multiplied together and the product is multiplied times the potential punishment, the expected cost is extremely small. The potential criminal's cost-benefit analysis therefore often implicitly shows that crime does indeed pay. In order to reduce criminal activities, including murder, an economist would argue that the price paid by the criminal must be increased.

[4] Peter Parsell and John R. Taylor, "The Deterrent Effect of Capital Punishment: Another View," *The American Economic Review*, vol. 67, no. 3 (June 1977), pp. 445–451.
[5] Gary Becker and William Landes, editors, *Essays in the Economics of Crime and Punishment* (Columbia University Press: New York, 1974).

DISCUSSION QUESTIONS

1. The analysis just presented makes the assumption that criminals act rationally. Does the fact that they do not necessarily do so negate our analysis?

2. In many cases, murder is committed among people who know each other. Does this mean that raising the price the murderer has to pay will not affect the quantity of murder demanded by perpetrators?

29

the economics of
The Future

Americans are currently confronted by conflicting views of the future. On one side, doomsday soothsayers predict that the end of the world, if not just around the corner, is certainly not far away. They foresee calamity coming from half a dozen different sources. On the other side, optimists propound the thesis that in the next 200 years we will live in a world of such abundance that scarcity will be a thing of the past, and our problem will be to adjust to a world of leisure in which the everyday acquisition of the necessities and even the luxuries of life will be a minor part of human existence. Which of these futurologist interpretations is correct? Let's begin by looking at the dismal side.

Perhaps the most widely known of the dismal forecasts is that of the Club of Rome. In the original Club of Rome study (1972), it was predicted that if the present growth trends in world population, industrialization, pollution, food production, and resource depletion continued unchanged, the limits to growth on this planet would be reached sometime in the next 100 years. The most probable result would be a rather sudden and uncontrollable decline in both population and industrial capacity. What are the sources of this dismal outlook? It comes first of all from examining the potential exhaustion of the world's basic supplies of energy sources and minerals. The Club of Rome predictions suggest that most of the known sources of energy, including petroleum, coal, and natural gas, will be exhausted within this 100-year span and that no currently unknown ones will take their place. This forecast is accompanied by an equally dismal prediction of population growth to approximately 15 billion from its current level of a little over 4 billion. The prospects indeed appear bleak.

But this is not the end of the gloomy forecasts. The Club of Rome predictions also stressed the inability to increase the food supply at a rate approaching that of the population growth, so that in the next 100 years famines and widespread disaster from lack of food will characterize the human condition. Indeed, we will be faced with the dilemma of who and what parts of the world we will simply let starve to death. Moreover, there are signs of ecological disaster in the growing pollution in the world, so that the oceans may become lifeless, devoid of fish or other sources of nutrition. We are faced with the possibility that the envelope that surrounds the earth in the stratosphere will be so polluted that there will be a change in the amount of sunlight that reaches the earth. Consequences could be increased radiation or a change in the temperature level of the earth so significant that human life may disappear. And we have not even talked yet about the possibilities of thermonuclear warfare. Given this scenario, the prospects for humankind are far from optimistic.

The opposite picture is offered by the more hopeful futurologists. In a book published in 1976 by the Hudson Institute entitled *The Next Two Hundred Years*, Herman Kahn argues that the likely future of humankind is rosy indeed. He predicts that by the year 2176, per capita income (in 1976 prices) will be almost $50,000 for the developed nations in the world and will be more than $10,000 per capita on the average for all people living in the world. This prediction is based on the view that the demographic transition is imminent—that is, that population is peaking at the current time and that the rate of increase will slow down in the future. Kahn is also optimistic about the potential supply of energy and mineral resources. He foresees that certain nonrenewable mineral resources, such as petroleum, have a much longer potential life than we now predict, and he reminds us that pessimistic projections about future reserves of petroleum have been promulgated ever since petroleum was first developed. These warnings about running out of petroleum have been sounded ever since Drake put down the first oil well in Titusville, Pennsylvania, more than a century ago. Moreover, when he looks at potential coal reserves, shale oil, and tar sands, Kahn sees an enormous potential supply of energy. He points out that the other basic minerals are in the same condition; that is, we have only begun to discover the reserves and even slight rises in the prices of these goods lead to the discovery of enormous supplies of additional potential resources. With respect to the food supply, he points to the existence of a great deal of arable land still left uncultivated in the world, and also to new techniques, such as the Green Revolution in Asia, which offer the promise of enormous increases in agricultural productivity. Finally, he offers an optimistic view of our efforts at pollution control and at preventing damage to the environment that would be antithetical to human survival. In Japan, for example, almost 2 percent of the Gross National Product is currently being used for antipollution efforts. Perhaps the most polluted of the advanced industrial nations, Japan is pointing up what will occur in the future.

While Kahn does not foreclose the possibility of ultimate human disaster, he nevertheless makes a strong case for the technological adaptability of human beings in the future to take into account and eliminate such possibilities.

These two studies, one pessimistic, the other optimistic, have been the subject of immense controversy. The Club of Rome partially repudiated its own study four years after publication. But in 1980 a study commissioned by President Carter, The Global 2000 Study, came out with many similar conclusions. Since the study had all the prestige of the United States government behind it, it received as much attention as the earlier Club of Rome study. Its dismal conclusion—that by the year 2000 we will face global calamity—was vigorously attacked by the optimists. Julian Simon, an economist at the University of Illinois, argued in a book entitled *The Ultimate Resource* that the assertions in that report are baseless and that the facts point in just the opposite direction.

Who is right in these contrasting scenarios of the future? Obviously, nobody knows for sure. Any predictions about the future must weigh such imponderables as thermonuclear warfare, side effects from the use of chemicals and pesticides, and other polluting effects of modern technology, currently unknown to us, which may suddenly produce disastrous consequences. If, however, we consider only the basic economic issues, leaving aside such imponderables, then the difference between these two positions rests on two fundamental questions about future development.

First, can we continue to develop new technology at constant cost that will lead to sustained economic growth? If we can, then we will be in a position to progressively develop substitutes for those resources that are potentially depletable. The experience of the last 75 years is consistent with such a pattern of development; that is, what we can observe in the past is that the rising price of any resource due to its relative scarcity leads to the profitability of developing substitutes for that resource. The evidence so far is consistent; that is, we do not observe a rising *real* price of natural resources. This evidence—no change in *real* price as opposed to *nominal* price—suggests that so far we have been successful in our endeavor to develop substitutes. The same holds true for agriculture and food supplies to the degree that we continue to revolutionize agricultural technology as we have in the past 100 years. We continue to stay ahead of the possibility of rising real prices of food, and the spectre of famine envisioned by that gloomy preacher Malthus almost 200 years ago has not materialized. In fact, current evidence suggests just the opposite.

Whereas in the United States in colonial times one farmer could feed 4 persons, today one farmer feeds 45 persons. In colonial times, almost all of our labor force was engaged in agriculture and produced just enough to feed us with a small amount left over for exports; in 1979 a little over 4 percent of our labor force was engaged in agriculture and managed not only to feed more than 220 million people, but also to make us one of the greatest agricultural exporting nations in the world. Surely this pattern suggests just the reverse of those dire predictions of famine.

But note the basic assumption at the beginning of this argument: What is necessary for this optimistic view to hold in the future is our continuous ability to devise new technologies at constant cost, as we have done in the past 100 years. The constant cost is the critical condition. If it takes more and more resources and effort to develop a new form of technology, then in the long run our future is indeed bleak. At this point we have no definitive assurance that we will continue to produce new technology; but neither do we have evidence to the contrary.

The second question relates to the future of population growth. If growth continues at the rate of the past century, then indeed we will face the prospect of a superpopulated world and ever more difficulty in keeping output and productivity ahead of population growth. In the less developed parts of the world, the rate of population increase has frequently been above 2 percent a year. If that rate continues, we can envision a world several hundred years hence in which people will literally be standing on each other's shoulders. But here, too, there is some reason for hope. In the last few years, for the first time there has been an actual decline in the rate of growth of population. If this is not an insignificant deviation in our long-run pattern but is in fact evidence of a fundamental change in the rate of population growth, then we may look forward to a meaningful slowdown.

A basic requirement for balancing population and productivity is to permit the signals provided by the price system to operate. There is no more fundamental lesson from history than the fact that human beings produce their own sources of decline and decay. Our discussion of the economics of wage and price controls (Chapter 7) is a reminder of this persistent tendency of human beings: in the face of immediate shortages, they will impose a set of controls that will not allow the price system to work. We have seen the consequences of such folly in the decay of housing in New York City. Yet despite this record, our knowledge is still conjectural. We have no real theory of political economy that would allow us to predict responses of human beings to changing relative prices.

SUMMARY

Gloom and doom predictions typically rely on extrapolation of physical data into the future. Historically, however, individuals have adapted to changes in relative prices that reflected changes in the relative scarcity of different resources. The more scarce a resource has become, the greater has been its relative price, and the price increase has caused consumers to cut back on their desired rate of consumption. More importantly, the increase in relative price has caused producers to find substitutes.

DISCUSSION QUESTIONS

1. Did the oil crisis of 1973–1974 support the Club of Rome argument?
2. Why should you be skeptical of both the Club of Rome and the Hudson Institute forecasts?

part five
Political Economy

INTRODUCTION

By now, you are certainly aware that many issues in our society have an economic basis. No matter what the economics of an issue may be, it probably has a political side, too. In fact, the subject matter of political economy is how the body politic decides on the allocation of resources. For the most part, political economy has as its basis different groups of individuals attempting to improve their economic position. Typically, a successful attempt by one group means that another group will suffer a deterioration in its economic position. Otherwise stated, the subject matter of political economy often involves a transfer of wealth among groups in society.

All the issues in this part are political in nature. An economic analysis of black economic progress, for example, reveals the political foundation of legislation aimed at helping members of minority groups. In the chapters on ecology and government programs, the explicit issue of income distribution is examined, and it is shown that many programs designed to improve the environment and help disadvantaged groups in fact end up improving the economic status of the middle classes and the well-to-do. Examining the issue of educational vouchers, we learn that those having the most to lose by experimenting with these vouchers are administrators and tenured instructors of relatively low quality who work in the public school systems. They, of course, will use their political clout, principally in the form of lobbying by the National Teachers Association, to prevent a wholesale switch from our current educational system to one utilizing vouchers. The chapters on Social Security and the negative income tax both point out the transfer of income and wealth that is occurring as a result of these systems. Once again, it is shown that groups continue to use political means to attempt to acquire more wealth for themselves.

Although politics plays a part in so many issues in our society, understanding the economic basis of political decisions can help one separate the reality from the rhetoric.

30

the economics of
Transport Deregulation

In 1987, we will celebrate the centenary of the establishment of the Interstate Commerce Commission (ICC), the first federal regulatory agency. For the last dozen years, federal regulation in general and transport regulation in particular have been under almost universal attack by both major political parties. President Carter made Alfred Kahn chairman of the Civil Aeronautics Board, and Kahn set about dismantling that agency's regulatory control. Ronald Reagan ran for office on a platform of wholesale deregulation of business and appointed as Chairman of his Council of Economic Advisers Murray Weidenbaum, who had made his reputation exposing the inefficiencies of government regulation. Are the days of the ICC numbered? Will it never reach its one hundredth birthday? Don't be too sure it won't. A little history will help us understand why.

It was at the behest of shippers that the ICC was established in the nineteenth century. But gradually the railroads discovered that the stability that had eluded them through rate agreements (which constantly broke down in periods of contraction) could be realized through the coercive power of government. In 1906, the Hepburn Act gave the ICC power to establish maximum rates, and in 1910, the Mann-Elkins Act established ICC control of telephone, telegraph and cable services. Eventually, as the truck became a competitor to the railroad, it too came under the control of the commission. Regulation of the airline industry evolved in the context of safety rather than (as in its early days) in the context of its role as competitor of the railroads. The Civil Aeronautics Board and the Federal Aviation Agency were the regulatory agencies in this case, but the results have been quite similar. The regulatory agency set rates, assigned routes, and had control over mergers, the selling or leasing of equipment, and so on. In short, the major decisions of private business firms—decisions made in response to consumer demand and competition of other firms—in the area of transport were now made by regulatory commissions.

Although firms in the regulated transport sector may have grumbled at the maze of red tape and the limits put upon their decision making, regulation had its advantages for them, too. Not only were rates set high enough to cover the costs of inefficient firms, but monopoly rents accrued to those firms that had favored (and exclusive) routes or exclusive certificates (in the trucking industry) for certain routes. Tom Moore estimated in 1978 that the value of such certificates and permits in the trucking industry was between $2 billion and $3 billion.[1]

It is not surprising that economists were broadly critical of the consequences of transport regulation. No matter where they looked, from the merchant marine to the movement of household goods, they found that the subsidies and restrictions were producing inefficient firms and monopoly profits. It is surprising, however, that the refrain was taken up by the major political par-

[1] Thomas Moore, "Beneficiaries of Trucking Regulation," *Journal of Law and Economics* (October 1978), pp. 327–343.

ties, and even more extraordinary that, under the stewardship of Alfred Kahn, the regulatory structure in the airline industry was dismantled piece by piece.

But that was in 1978. In 1982, the economy was experiencing a major recession: Braniff, one of the major airlines, went bankrupt; other airlines showed a sea of red ink and, indeed, some may follow Braniff. Laker Airways, which had pioneered cheap North Atlantic fares in the face of the international cartel (the International Air Transport Association), also went bankrupt. World Airways, which had led the movement toward lower fares, asked the CAB to "end the disastrous and completely irrational fare wars."[2]

As a result, the administration proposed legislation to exempt from antitrust laws maritime industry agreements on rates, profit sharing, cargo sharing, and capacity limitations.[3] As for the trucking industry, the Teamsters Union had been the lone supporter of Ronad Reagan among large trade unions, and it had shared with the industry in the dividing up of the monopoly profits. As could be expected, the Teamsters had vigorously opposed deregulation and, not surprisingly, little progress has been made in the way of deregulation.

To the economist, deregulation of transportation means increased efficiency; to the consumer, it means lower fares and better services. To firms in the industries, deregulation means increased competition, lower profits, no cushion to prevent bankruptcy, and a continuous struggle; to politicians, it is something that requires lip service since it is a popular issue. But politicians are caught in a dilemma, since they are faced with quiet but relentless (and well-funded) pressure from firms and trade unions to do something about "disastrous and destructive competition."

The issue is straightforward. Economists view competition as the key to an efficient economic system; they can offer endless examples to illustrate the inefficiency associated with monopoly and cartels, whether private or governmental. But is competition

[2] *Wall Street Journal*, July 27, 1982.
[3] Ibid.

a viable long-run form of organization? Economists may applaud it, consumers may benefit from it, and politicians may pay lip service to it. But who wants to be a participant in the uncertain world of a competitive industry? Not business, not farmers, not trade unions. For all of them, there is a way out. If competition cannot be reduced through voluntary "cooperation," it can be reduced through government intervention. This is a story without an ending because the outcome is in doubt. But we wouldn't bet against the survival of the ICC to the ripe old age of 100.

SUMMARY

A complete analysis of most regulation in the transportation field shows that it has served to benefit specific groups in society—and usually not the consumer. In the past, under an era of regulation, the owners of the rights to provide transportation services reaped monopoly profits. One of the major effects of regulation of transportation has been inefficiency in the use of resources due to numerous strictures. Economists have long argued for more competition in transportation to reduce these inefficiencies. The issue is political, however. To the extent that industries that were regulated in the past succeed in keeping some form of regulation today, they may succeed through political means in reestablishing much of the discarded regulation of the past.

DISCUSSION QUESTIONS

1. Discuss the way in which monopoly profits develop through regulatory action.
2. Why would some politicians favor deregulation and others favor regulation?

31

the economics of
British Rail

The post-World War II economic history of Great Britain is a familiar story of the relative economic decline of a great nation. After the war, Britain was left without an empire and the country that was the originator of modern economic growth became relatively stagnant. In the 38 years since the end of World War II, most of the Western European countries have surpassed Britain in living standards. Britain is universally held up as the classic modern case of economic stagnation. What happened? It is a more complicated story than we can tell in a few pages, but the economics of the British Rail is a piece of the story.

      Britain, in comparison with America, is a small, very compact, densely settled nation. The railroad was invented there and in the almost 160 years since its inception, a dense railroad network has developed to carry freight and passengers to every corner of the British Isles. New technological developments invented by the Japanese and the French have increased the speed and comfort of rail travel, and the high-speed computer has made possible automated systems for the operation of freight and passenger movement. The railroad can hold its own against other forms of transportation. In a country the size and density of Britain, it would appear to be the ideal basic transport system. To quote the *London Times*, "Railroads provide the most civilized way of travelling and transporting freight—faster, safer, more reliable and less of a nuisance to others than most alternative kinds of transport; cheaper than the car, and far better placed in the future to make convenient use of energy resources as oil runs out." In short, the advertising logo of British Rail, "This is the age of the train," would appear to be justified. Moreover, British Rail is a government-run enterprise. If it runs a deficit, it can simply appeal to the government to provide a subsidy. In 1982 that subsidy was well in excess of $1 billion. But far from being a thriving industry, British Rail is in deep trouble. Private cars alone now account for more than ten times as many passenger miles as the railways, and motor coaches are steadily eating into the long-distance passenger service. Eighty-five percent of freight traffic now moves by road and, in contrast to the rest of Europe, Britain actually is now moving less freight by rail than at any other time in this century.

In the winter of 1982, one of the two rail unions, Amalgamated Society of Locomotivemen, Engineers, and Firemen (ASLEF), engaged in a devastating three-days-a-week (Tuesday, Thursday, and Saturday) strike, which cost British Rail a large sum and led to further long-term losses of passengers and freight. ASLEF was striking against "flexible rostering," that is, the right of the railroad to adjust the length of time a member of ASLEF worked. Instead of a rigid 8 hours, the worker would have a variable 7–9 hour schedule; in return, however, the workweek would be reduced from 40 to 39 hours. The issue was productivity. With a rigid 8-hour schedule, a train driver of ASLEF actually worked an average of 3 hours and 20 minutes a day. The rest of his time was used to get to another place to drive another train. With flexible rostering, the railroad could adjust train drivers to trains and hence get more *actual* useful working time.

The issue is symptomatic of the long-run struggle between the two unions, the National Union of Railwaymen (NUR) and ASLEF, and British Rail. Featherbedding and make-work are a way of life of the unions. The unions fear—and rightly so—that methods that increase productivity will lead to a reduction in workers and hence more unemployment for their members; they therefore resist such measures. British Rail is convinced that unless it increases productivity, it will continue to lose out to its competitors in transportation. But the issue goes deeper than that. At stake is the basic institutional structure of the British economy.

Let's forget the subsidy for a minute. In order to cover its costs, British Rail must charge enough for passengers and freight so as not to lose money. But if its costs per passenger mile and per ton mile (for freight) stay constant, with no change in productivity, but keep dropping in competitive transport, the railroad must either lose out to competitors or drop its prices.

For the union, there are two possible solutions to this problem. One is the American way—to extend regulatory control over competitive forms of transportation to prevent them from lowering their prices (see Chapter 30, The Economics of Transport Deregulation). The other is the solution adopted by British trade unions—subsidize the railroad. Simply make up the difference between revenue and cost by a grant from the government each year. But that requires a government willing to underwrite increasingly large expenditures.

The trade unions are the backbone of the Labour Party in Britain, and since 1945, the Labour Party has been in power off and on. Its policies have included nationalization of many industries and, when such industries lost money, subsidization by government. Subsidies come from tax revenues, so there has been a redistribution of income from taxpayers to the industry. In effect, the industries' consumers are being subsidized. Passengers and shippers of freight on British Rail pay lower prices for tickets or tariffs for freight than would have been the case in the absence of the subsidy. But the ultimate beneficiaries are the members of NUR and ASLEF, since the evidence above suggests that the industry demand curve is quite elastic. Therefore at the nonsubsidized prices, there would be an even more rapid decline in the use of the railroad and, thus, of railroad employment.

The other major political party[1]—the Conservative Party —has generally reflected the views of disgruntled taxpayers. Currently in power, the Conservatives have refused a further bailout of British Rail or an increase in the subsidy. As of this writing, the issues are still up in the air. In June 1982, the NUR went on strike only to have its executive board rescind the strike when approximately 30 percent of its members showed up for work anyway. Then in July, ASLEF went on strike—still over flexible rostering—but finally agreed to consider the new method of scheduling. But if British Rail has won some skirmishes, the basic issues are still unsettled. The unions believe that permitting the introduction of new technology means the substitution of capital for labor—and therefore unemployment for their members and a decline in the power and strength of the unions. Their solution would be either to prevent competition or, when that is impossible, to subsidize the wages (and therefore employment) of the worker. British Rail feels that it must increase productivity to survive and the taxpayer (not to mention the commuter) feels that he or she should not be paying tribute to ASLEF and the NUR. While the economics of British Rail is only a small part of the story of the relative decline of Britain, it highlights the basic issues. Those issues are economic, but their resolution will be political. Political economy is, after all, the real name of the game.

SUMMARY

Regulation of one mode of transportation without regulation of other modes will lead to the competitive disadvantage of the reg-

[1] Actually, as of this writing, there is another major political party—the Social Democratic Party—made up largely of disgruntled members of the Labour Party who feel that party has moved too far to the left. The new party has made an alliance with the Liberal Party (a relatively minor party) to become a third major political party.

ulated mode. That is what has happened to British Rail. If the rest of transportation is not regulated, subsidies must be granted to the regulated form in order to keep it alive. Such subsidies come from general tax revenues and involve a redistribution of income from taxpayers to the industry. In effect, the consumers of British Rail services have been subsidized by all taxpayers. However, the main beneficiaries of such subsidies are the members of the railroad unions.

DISCUSSION QUESTIONS

1. Is it "rational" for British trade unions to fight technological change?
2. What determines the elasticity of demand for rail services?

32

the economics of
Ecology and Income Distribution

There are few more unsightly aspects to the urban environment than the jungle of poles and overhead wires that foul the typical cityscape. When we extend the term "pollution" to include visual pollution, overhead wires are a prime candidate for inclusion in this category. The solution is to place them underground, and this process is going on in many cities around the United States.

Typically, the relocating of arterial wiring is paid for by a general rate increase; but in residential areas, it is not uncommon for the citizens of an area who want this change to form a Local Improvement District (an LID), develop a plan, and submit it to the appropriate body for approval. Usually the utility company pays part of the cost, and each lot owner pays a proportionate share of the rest (in Seattle, the ratio has been approximately 50–50). Placing wires underground in an already developed residential area is expensive, with the total amounting to as much as

$2200 per lot. It is not surprising that this type of cost sharing has tended to restrict most underground wiring to higher-income areas. However, since the share paid for by the utility company comes from the general income received from everyone's rates, while benefits accrue to the upper-income groups, such projects reflect a redistribution of income from poor to rich.

Two options exist. We could insist that the lot owner pay the entire cost of placing wiring underground, in which case there would be no redistribution but also, probably, very little change. Or, we could let the utility company raise rates sufficiently to alter the wiring of the whole city, in which case everyone would pay. At a recent public hearing on the subject in Seattle, the head of the local utility company testified that such a program stretching over a ten-year period would necessitate a doubling of electricity rates. A rate increase bears more heavily on the poor because the percentage of their income that goes for electricity is typically greater than the percentage for the rich. Thus the consequence is again to impose a greater relative burden on the poor than the rich. Is the case of underground wiring different in its effects on income distribution from other solutions to environmental problems?

Before we attempt to answer this difficult question, we reiterate a fact of which all readers should now be well aware. Every action has a cost. That is, every action involves some opportunity cost, whether or not this cost is explicitly stated or even understood by those incurring it. Since our world is one of limited resources, it is also a world of tradeoffs. In the underground-wiring example, we can trade off higher electric rates (or smaller amounts of income to spend on other things) for beauty (no overhead wires). Beauty does not come to us free of charge. When it is realized that every alternative course of action involves certain sets of costs, then it is time to ask, "Who will bear these costs?" We have already seen what happened in one case. We can now discuss others.

Many citizens are attempting to have forest areas preserved as pure wilderness, arguing that we should preserve as much of our *natural* ecology (as opposed to that made by humans) as possible. Preserving wilderness areas involves costs and benefits. The costs include less forest area for other purposes, such as camping grounds and logging. Who bears these costs? People who like to camp (but not backpack) in the first case, and people who buy houses and other wood products,[1] in the second.

Although the reader can easily understand the first case, the second may not be so obvious. Look at it this way. When fewer forest areas are used for logging, the supply of lumber is smaller than it would be otherwise.[2] With any given demand (schedule) the price of lumber will therefore be higher than otherwise, and houses become more expensive.[3]

Now for the benefits. Wilderness-area preservation offers benefits to those who like backpacking in the preserved area, and to those who can enjoy fishing and hunting there. Benefits are also bestowed upon those who do not themselves backpack, hunt, or fish, but who would pay something to keep the wilderness for their children.

To determine what effect the saving of a natural ecology area has on the distribution of income, broadly defined, we have therefore tried to discover, as always, who bears the costs and who obtains the benefits. This is usually an empirical question, which can be answered only by examining relevant data. From limited studies that have been done, we can make a tentative conclusion about wilderness preservation. It has been found that backpackers are, in general, well educated and earn considerably more than the average. Thus the gains from that activity go to middle- and upper-income groups. As for who bears the costs, we know that campers (those with tents, trailers, and camper-trucks) are, on the average, less well educated than backpackers and earn considerably less. Hence, we are trading off recreation facilities used by lower-income people in favor of those used by higher-income people.

[1] Or wood-product substitutes, for that matter.
[2] The supply schedule is farther to the left.
[3] Note that the same is also true for nonwood houses. If the price of wood houses is higher than otherwise, more people will substitute nonwood houses—and their price will be bid up (their demand schedule shifts outward to the right).

As for the increased price of housing due to less lumber, we know that the poor will suffer more than the rich, because housing expenditures are a larger fraction of the poor's budget.

We can easily take other examples. Question: Should the level of a dam be raised to provide more hydroelectric power, or should the virgin timber area around it be left a wilderness area for backpackers? As economists, we cannot answer the question. We can merely point out all of the costs and benefits associated with two (or more) alternatives. In this example, the costs (in ecological terms) of raising the dam level would be borne largely by actual and potential backpackers. The benefits would be lower electricity rates and/or the saving of resources that would have been needed to develop an alternative source of energy supply. If electricity payments represent a larger fraction of the income of the poor than the rich, raising the level of the dam might redistribute income from the rich to the poor. We say "might," because the income is redistributed only if the poor pay less relative to what they get.

There is, of course, a way of preserving our ecology without redistributing income.[4] The government could institute user charges for such things as wilderness areas and hunting preserves, setting them to cover the imputed opportunity cost of the resources being used. The totals collected could then be redistributed in a manner that would compensate those bearing the costs.

SUMMARY

Improving the environment is costly, and the benefits are seldom evenly distributed. We need to carefully analyze the distribution of the costs and benefits of alternative programs to see who benefits and who pays.

DISCUSSION QUESTIONS

1. Why aren't user charges imposed?
2. What would be the distributional consequences of installing catalytic converters in all new automobiles?

[4] But not without redistributing the use of resources.

33

the economics of
Black
Economic
Progress

In the past 20 years, the federal government has attempted, by the legislative process, to reduce racial discrimination against blacks. How effective has this legislation been? Indeed, can equal opportunity be legislated? According to Richard Freeman of Harvard University, the Civil Rights Act of 1964 has been a major factor in reducing discrimination and improving the lot of black wage earners. In reviewing the findings of Freeman, and of James Heckman and Richard Butler of the University of Chicago, we find that they reach a far more cautious appraisal of the importance of legislation in improving black economic welfare. While they agree that it appears likely that young blacks have fared better as a result of antidiscrimination legislation, citing the increase in school enrollment rates as a case in point, they nevertheless conclude that for blacks as a whole the issue is still undetermined.

There is agreement that substantial black economic progress occurred between 1964 and 1975. The more spectacular gains have been made by black women. In 1964, the median wage or salary for black women was 58 percent of the median for white women. By 1975 it had risen to 97 percent. Moreover, the status of black women's jobs has also improved substantially. For black male workers, the age and level of skill made an important difference in the degree to which they had caught up. In 1964, young black workers aged 20–24 earned 68 percent of what young white workers earned. By 1975 the figure was 85 percent. For older workers, the progress has been slower. Comparable figures were 65 percent in 1964 and 70 percent in 1975. The most spectacular success for males has been among highly qualified blacks. Black professionals in 1964 earned 69 percent of what comparable whites did, but by 1975 this figure had gone up to 84 percent. And for Ph.D.s, as well as recent graduates with a bachelor's degree in business, blacks appeared to do approximately as well in the mid-1970s as comparable whites. These are spectacular gains, and they stem from the passage of the Civil Rights Act of 1964. Freeman argues that the 1964 act shifted the demand curve to the right for blacks; he uses a mass of statistics to support the fact that it was this piece of legislation that altered the opportunity of blacks.

Heckman and Butler, on the other hand, using the same time series analysis and econometric techniques, conclude that the evidence does not show that there has been a shift to the right in the demand curve, but instead, primarily a shift to the left in the supply curve. Their argument is that social expenditures on welfare in the late 1960s led to a reduction in labor force participation rates among low-wage workers — those most likely to participate in social welfare programs. Since there had been a much greater share of blacks in this low-wage group than of whites, the consequence was to relatively reduce the supply of black workers in the labor force. According to Heckman and Butler, with a reduced supply of black workers at the low end of the scale, the relative wage of those blacks who remained in the labor force was clearly raised. The key to their findings is that if market demand had shifted favorably for blacks, it should have resulted in an increase in the labor force participation rate. But, in fact, just the reverse happened; that is, the participation rate of blacks has declined. Heckman and Butler believe this finding is inconsistent with the shift in demand to the right which Freeman argues is a result of the Civil Rights Act. For Heckman and Butler, the most important source of improved well-being for blacks has been the remarkable change in the American South due to improving school quality, industrialization, and out-migration from the South.

How far apart are these two positions? Heckman and Butler concede that perhaps legislation has had some impact, particularly on young blacks, as mentioned earlier. And surely the improvement in schooling in the South, together with somewhat more readiness to employ blacks, is, if not directly, at least indirectly tied to legislative activity. Nevertheless, the differences in these positions are important since they call into question the degree of effectiveness of direct legislation in prohibiting discrimination. The answer is still unclear; but it should be pointed out that whichever side one takes, the dilemma of black welfare is still not altogether resolved. Both Freeman and Heckman and Butler make clear that the participation rate of blacks in the labor force is lower than that of whites; that is, unemployment among young blacks is much higher than among whites. Hence, the problem of how a society can create equality of opportunity still remains.

SUMMARY

There appears to have been substantial black economic progress between 1964 and 1975. Two alternative reasons have been given. One is that the demand curve for blacks has shifted outward to the right because of the 1964 Civil Rights Act. An opposing view maintains that the supply curve of blacks has shifted to the left because welfare programs have reduced the labor force participation rate among blacks. Proponents of the second view argue that the major sources of improved black well-being are improved school quality, industrialization of the American South, and out-migration from the South.

DISCUSSION QUESTIONS

1. How would an increase in social welfare programs lead to a reduction in the labor force participation rate of minority groups?
2. Why have we observed out-migration of blacks from the South to the North?

34

the economics of
Educational Vouchers

Everywhere we turn there is dissatisfaction with the performance of the school system. School levies fail frequently; school teachers go out on strike; and students are bored silly by the system. When the idea of educational vouchers first appeared in the 1970s, it seemed to be the ideal answer to the malaise that affects the school system. The idea was simple. Instead of giving money to public schools, with each child being assigned to a school (or alternatively occasioning outlays for private schools), vouchers would be given directly to families so that they could enroll children in schools of their choice. The idea had particular appeal for reformers who viewed the ghetto schools as an issue, since it offered parents alternatives to the poor education provided by the public school system. Catholics liked the idea because the vouchers would boost enrollment in parochial schools. Believers in the free market felt that it was the answer, since it provided a system of free choice in the educational world analogous to the market system in the economic world. The appeal of vouchers was that they would encourage competition, which would thereby shake up the school system and force it to be more attentive to the diverse needs that an educational system should satisfy. In short, the voucher system appeared to be the economist's ideal answer to a complex question.

But the voucher system met a storm of protest from inside and outside the educational establishment. Teachers viewed it as a way of union busting; administrators were afraid that they would lose control over budgets and appointments; and liberals felt that the flow of monies to sectarian schools would threaten the separation of church and state. Moreover, while the proposed plan provided freedom of choice, the voucher system would destroy the egalitarian principles of schooling since rich parents could supplement the amount of the voucher and send their children to more expensive schools, while poor parents could not. Thus the simple economics of the voucher system were placed in direct confrontation with the political economy of the system, reflecting the vested interests and views of groups that saw their values threatened.

Still, in the face of widespread opposition, the idea persisted and led the federal government to solicit school systems to try out the voucher system. However, since school systems usually were intransigent in their opposition, the federal government found it difficult to find a school system that would try the experiment. The little district of Alum Rock in California, however, was in poor financial condition, and its superintendent felt that any experiment could not help but ameliorate the multiple problems he faced.

What happened when Alum Rock tried the voucher system? Did more educational diversity result? Did the schools become more responsive to the will of the parents? Did the power of professionals wane? Competition among schools should have led to enrollment increases in programs that were appealing to parents and to unemployment for unpopular teachers who taught poorly. But the school professionals' first objective was to protect their jobs. Accordingly, it was immediately agreed that any teacher who left a voucher school for reasons associated with the experiment would be given priority in assignments to other schools. No one would be put out on the street. This decision eased things for unpopular teachers, but even for successful teachers the results were a mixed blessing. Although their schools received more tuition, the monies were spent for more teachers and untested materials, consequently increasing the everyday problems of teachers struggling with more planning, more meetings, and more colleagues. Professionals put a halt to extensive redistribution by imposing a ceiling on enrollments in schools. The result was that once a school reached its enrollment capacity, the spillover was, of necessity, returned to the less popular schools. School principals were particularly sensitive to any comparative testing that might have evaluated their relative performances; hence, comparative evaluations that would draw attention to differences and encourage parents to change schools were discouraged. In short, the program strayed a long way from the intentions of the original authors of the system.

Did parents respond to the new ability to make choices? Some did, and indeed by the third year, approximately 18 percent of parents had chosen to send their children to schools outside the neighborhood. But the percentage was still small and reflected the passivity of most parents in the face of professionals. However, it would be a mistake to imagine that nothing did happen; in fact, greater diversity within the schools did emerge. Where before there had been a uniform curriculum, now there were Spanish-English bilingual programs, an arts and crafts minischool, and several open classrooms. In short, more innovation had taken place. Finally, it should be recognized that everyone knew that the Alum Rock experiment was a temporary one and that it would come to an end. Therefore, the degree to which it reflected the experience that might have taken place under permanent conditions was very limited indeed.

What can be learned from the Alum Rock experiment? First of all, by and large parents did not exercise much more choice than before. The power of school administrators and professionals emerged undiminished and, indeed, may have increased. On the other hand, there is no doubt that the experiment promoted diversity among schools and encouraged further experimentation. Nevertheless, the entrenched position of teacher and administrator groups led the experiment far from the original intentions of those who wished to impose the conditions of the market on the school system.

Whether one evaluates this experiment as a success or a failure, it shows how the simple economics of choice applied to an institutional structure can be modified by the realities of political economy, in which vested interests alter the way the market is permitted to work.

SUMMARY

Under a system of educational vouchers, competition will cause a larger variety of schooling environments to exist. If public schools were allowed to co-exist with private schools under the educational voucher system, public schools would have to provide services of equal quality to private schools. Not surprisingly, public school officials have routinely fought the implementation of an educational voucher system.

DISCUSSION QUESTIONS

1. In most metropolitan areas, a wide variety of nursery schools exist. Some specialize in art, some in dance, some in scholastic training, and others in sports. Once the child reaches kindergarten or first-grade age, however, the choice of schools becomes much less varied. Why?
2. Would a system of educational vouchers necessarily mean the death of the public school system?

35

the economics of

Income Distribution and Government Programs

As has been done in many countries, our government has instituted programs for helping sectors of the economy where aid seems to be needed. In most cases, the implicit aim of these various programs is to effect a redistribution of income.

As pointed out in Chapter 32, all programs to improve or maintain our environment involve both costs and benefits. This is true of any government program. If we are to understand the actual, as opposed to the avowed, redistributional aspects of any governmental policy, we must fully assess the range of costs and benefits. Also, once again, we must determine empirically who bears these costs and benefits.

Let us examine the redistributional effects of the farm program. The obvious intent of this program is to maintain farmers' incomes at a level that society feels is acceptable (that is, not "too" low). The questions to be asked are: (1) Does the program fulfill that purpose? Who reaps the benefits? and (2) How is the program paid for?—who incurs the costs?

To answer the latter question first: All direct and indirect government outlays for the farm program come directly out of government revenues. Taxpayers share in these costs in proportion to the percentage of total receipts they contribute.[1] Direct costs of price supports, surplus storage, and soil banks added up to $9 billion in 1982. Indirect costs confront the consumer every time he or she buys a sack of potatoes, in the form of artificially raised prices. It is obvious that the explicit aim of price supports is just that—to support the prices of farm crops above the levels they would have attained under free competition. Comparably, the announced aim of soil banks is "conservation," but one effect is to reduce the supply of cultivated lands and hence the supply of crops offered for sale. To the extent that conservation succeeds, the prices of farm products are higher than they would otherwise be. The aim of crop control and marketing quotas is to reduce the supply of the crop that is put onto the market for sale; again, the result is higher prices.

Who bears the costs of higher prices? Consumers bear these costs directly, in proportion to the quantity of farm products they buy. It is an empirical fact that the poor spend a larger fraction of their incomes on food than do the rich.[2] We may, therefore, view the farm programs' resultant higher food prices as a regressive system of taxes that causes a redistribution of income, since the poor pay relatively more for what they get than the rich do.

Who benefits from the farm program? The benefits of higher prices are directly proportional to the amount of farm products sold; therefore, on average, the benefits are *directly*

---

[1] Taxpayers contribute both directly, via income taxes, and indirectly, via the income they use to buy products whose prices are higher because the manufacturer also pays taxes.

[2] That is, the income elasticity for food as a whole is less than unity. The German scholar Ernest Engel systematically documented this fact in 1857, and it is now known as Engel's law. As an example, in 1955 nonfarm families with a per capita income of $2000 spent 27 percent of their incomes on food. Families with a per capita income of $600 spent 46 percent.

proportional to a farmer's income.[3] The benefits resulting from governmental buying of "surpluses" are directly proportional to the amount of surpluses sold by a farmer. In general, this indicates that benefits are proportional to farmers' incomes, since those producing and selling more crops usually derive higher incomes. By the same reasoning, the benefits of the soil-bank program are directly proportional to the number of acres not cultivated. The larger the farm, the larger the amount that can be included in the soil bank and the larger the benefits—which once more are thus positively related to a farmer's income.

A few statistics should prove persuasive. About 10 percent of U.S. farmers produce 80 to 90 percent of the crops marketed. In 1980, farmers earning $100,000 or more received about 60 percent of their total incomes from direct governmental payments, rent, and dividends. The figure for farmers with incomes of less than $5000 was a mere 6.9 percent.

After weighing the costs and benefits of our farm program, one can only conclude that its effect is apparently to redistribute income from the poor to the relatively less poor. Of course this assertion would be invalidated if it could be shown that the poor pay proportionately lower taxes toward governmental expenditures than do the rich.

A similar analysis can be applied to the sugar import quota. In the past couple of years the world price of sugar has dropped by half. In the United States, however, stable prices have continued despite the world price drop and domestic recession. This is because domestic producers are protected from world competition by an import quota system. The gainers are those who owned

[3] Note, though, that if there is free entry into farming, higher prices will induce an increase in the amount of resources devoted to farming. Diminishing returns to incremental factors of production in agriculture ensure that in the long run, and with free entry, higher farm prices will not benefit all farmers (unless, of course, the government is buying surpluses and continues to pay for more and more soil banks and the like). With diminishing marginal returns to factors of production, per unit costs rise as output is expanded. Hence, high farm prices merely lead to more output until the additional costs of production just match the additional revenue received for the output. At that point, only farmers with specialized talents will be earning more than a normal profit.

beet and cane sugar land at the time of the passage of the bill establishing the quotas. The losers are consumers paying higher prices for sugar. And since low-income families do much of their own canning and preserving, it is likely that they bear a disproportionate burden of the government program.

Turning now to our income tax system, let us consider how certain tax deductions redistribute income. An individual paying off a home mortgage is allowed to deduct the interest payments. This is an incentive for home ownership, since buyers benefit by not having to apply their marginal tax rate to that amount of income. Ms. A, whose annual mortgage interest payments equal $1000 and whose marginal tax rate is 20 percent will gain $200 in income that does not have to be handed over to the government. Splendid! But consider the case of Mr. B., who earns twice the salary of Ms. A, and is in the 40 percent tax bracket. For the $2000 he paid out as interest this year, which he deducts from his income tax, he saves $400. The rich individual with a mortgaged home has benefited more than a less rich person in the same situation, and far more than a poor individual whose marginal tax rate is zero, or than anyone who has no mortgage payments on which to receive concessions.

We have already considered the ways in which income is redistributed by laws which make prostitution and narcotics illegal. In both cases we can say that, since information is more costly for illegal goods and services, in general those who can afford to pay more (the wealthy) receive a "better" product than those who are poor.

We can also recall the questions of rent controls and usury laws. If laws controlling usury and rents are effective, they establish a price below the market-clearing price. Dealers in apartments and credit therefore look for nonpecuniary returns when selling their products. Who is a better credit risk, a person who makes $20,000 per year or a person who works off and on for about $5000 a year? At the same rate of interest, a lender will give funds to the former and not to the latter. The poor get very few loans indeed when usury laws are enforced.

Under rent control, will the landlord rent to a welfare recipient or to the daughter of a city council member? At the same price, he will probably rent to the latter, since she is more likely to make her rent payments regularly.

All of these examples are given to illustrate the need to examine the distribution of the costs and benefits of government programs, and to decide whether they actually redistribute income in the intended direction. To the contrary, it appears that many policies tend to favor the rich at the expense of the less rich. However, this assumption must be verified anew for any prospective program.

SUMMARY

An analysis of many government programs shows that they do not benefit poor people, as generally intended. For example, any farm program that involves price supports and the like benefits farmers in proportion to their output. Poor farmers are, by definition, those who do not have large output. Therefore, richer farmers benefit the most from government farm programs. As a general proposition, many government programs tend to benefit others than the very poor in our society.

DISCUSSION QUESTIONS

1. Discuss a government program that favors the poor.
2. On balance, what are the distributional consequences of federal government tax and expenditure programs?

36

the economics of
Smoking

Recently, a California woman asked a bus driver to stop several youths from smoking on the bus. He did so, and as she was leaving the bus one youth spit in her face, hit her on the head, and fled. At about the same time in Seattle, Washington, a young man told a woman sitting beside him in a bus that he objected to smoking and asked her to put out her cigarette. When she failed to do so, he plucked the cigarette from her mouth and ground it out on her dress. The bitter resentment that has grown up between smoker and nonsmoker manifests itself on an everyday basis.

Twenty years ago smoking existed everywhere; indeed, it was something of a status symbol to smoke. Television ads and movies showed the heroes and heroines dangling cigarettes from their mouths. All that has changed. The beginning of that change can be dated from the 1964 Surgeon General's report, which made clear that smoking is harmful to one's health. Most recently, in an addendum to that report published on January 11, 1979, the Surgeon General added that the death rate from lung cancer had risen astronomically. An estimated 21,900 women and 70,000 men died from lung cancer in 1978, compared to a total of 45,838 lung cancer deaths in 1964.

But the issue here is not one of the right of individuals to pursue their own self-destruction by smoking. It is a straightforward issue of externalities. Smoking is obnoxious to nonsmokers; and, whereas in the past the smokers assumed they could smoke wherever they pleased, they can no longer take this for granted. Some, perhaps even many, nonsmokers (perhaps a better word would be antismokers) are violent in their opposition to smoking in their presence. Whether smoking physically harms nonsmokers who are in physical proximity to smokers is a still-debated question. Certainly it does not do them any good, and it probably harms those with respiratory diseases or allergies. Most studies indicate that the harm is probably small in terms of physical effects, but there can be no doubt that smoking is irritating to the nonsmoker, and more particularly, to the ex-smoker. No one is more zealous at preventing smoking than an individual like Joseph Califano, former Secretary of Health, Education and Welfare, who used to smoke and has now become a strong supporter of preventing smoking.

Smoking, as we have said, is a classic case of an externality, one in which it would be appropriate for the smoker to compensate the nonsmoker for the discomfort felt—according to the efficiency standards of the economist. Or, in the absence of compensation, the correct policy might be to impose rules and regulations that prevent the smoker from being able to irritate the nonsmoker. For example, the Civil Aeronautics Board has now mandated that nonsmokers must be separated from smokers on commercial air transports. Our story would be simple if it ended there—just another externality case to be solved by government policies. But the government's position is not that unequivocal. What the government does with its left hand—the hand of HEW and the Surgeon General, which has resulted in warnings on all packages of cigarettes of the danger to one's health, and in a heavily subsidized publicity campaign to prevent smoking—is countered by its right hand—the Department of Agriculture's subsidies to the tobacco industry. The approximately 500,000 growers of tobacco in the United States are prevented from competition by laws that do not allow increased acreage and that provide a prohibitive tax of 75 percent on all tobacco grown on unlicensed land. The result is to provide monopoly returns to those growers fortunate enough to have been in on the beginning of this subsidy (which started some three decades ago).

There's still more to the right hand of government. Tax receipts from the sale of cigarettes in 1981 approximated $13 billion. These included federal, state, and local taxes as well as receipts from import duties on tobacco and tobacco products. Tobacco and tobacco products contributed $2.4 billion to the plus side of the American balance of payments in 1981. Clearly, some parts of the federal government feel that they have a great deal to gain from the continued use of tobacco. So does the subsidized farmer in the American South, who is receiving direct returns from the monopoly granted to tobacco growing and supported by the Department of Agriculture.

On the other hand, the costs in terms of mortality and morbidity from cigarette smoking are large and they are rising. Estimates of the costs of medical care ranged as high as $11.5 billion in 1974. Furthermore, cigarette smoking has turned out to be a major fire hazard in modern times. National Fire Protection Association statistics suggest that 56 percent of fatal residential fires are a result of smoking. In 1981, smoking caused at least 94,000 fires and $246.4 million in property damages. And so it goes.

Should we ban smoking? An economist is in no position to answer that question. The economist can point out the costs and benefits involved and measure the externalities involved, but ultimately the issue becomes one of political economy. There can be no doubt that if smoking were discovered for the first time today, it would be put in the same class as cocaine, heroin, and dangerous drugs and considered something that should be outlawed by society. But smoking grew up to be a national craze in an era when it coincided with a prestige value, and it still retains much of that aura for young people. And obviously smokers are voters, too, as are tobacco growers, and the growing legions of antismokers. As a result, it is not surprising that the politics of smoking should lead to contradictory roles in government — where the left hand works to prohibit smoking and the right hand to promote it.

SUMMARY

Problems related to smoking are both internal and external. Internal problems involve self-infliction of such diseases as lung cancer. External problems involve polluting the air that others breathe. Since air is common property, there is no a priori reason to argue that nonsmokers have more rights to clean air than smokers have rights to pollute the air. A decision to prohibit smoking imposes a cost on smokers; a decision to allow smoking imposes a cost on nonsmokers. The argument is symmetric because air is common property.

DISCUSSION QUESTIONS

1. Is there a similarity between the analysis of smoking and the analysis of the use of wilderness areas by motorcycle riders?
2. Some researchers maintain that the smoke inhaled by nonsmokers creates as much (or more) danger of lung cancer as the smoke directly inhaled by smokers. If these researchers are correct, does this mean that smoking should not be allowed in public places?

37

the economics of
The
Social Security
Program

Protection against the insecurities associated with employment disability and old age has been a concern of government since early times. However, comprehensive coverage by a government to replace the extended family system began with Germany's initiation of a modern social security program in 1883. In the United States it was not until 1935, in the depths of the Depression, that the federal government passed the Social Security Law and created the system which is the basis of today's social security system. At the inception of the system, the basic issue was whether social security should be insurance, in the sense that insurance is built on the principle of an actuarially sound reserve that would allow payment of potential claims, or a system in which current employees pay for the benefits of those who are retired. As initiated in 1935, social security constituted a compromise between these positions: taxes were collected beginning in 1937, but no benefits were to be paid until 1942 so that a reserve could be accumulated. The original tax was 1 percent of employees' salaries, with another 1 percent coming from employers; this tax was levied on the first $3000 of an individual's wages. Gradually, the tax rate went up and the wage base increased.

Until 1960, receipts from taxes exceeded expenditures; accordingly, a reserve trust fund accumulated. From 1965 onward, Congress has been extremely generous in increasing payments to social security recipients. Monthly benefits were increased across the board by 7 percent in 1965, 13 percent in 1967, 15 percent in 1969, 10 percent in 1971, 20 percent in 1972, and 5.9 percent during the first half of 1973. Before the 5.9 percent increase had become effective in June of 1974, it was replaced by an even higher increase of 11 percent; and in June of 1975 another 8 percent cost-of-living adjustment was made. Whatever compromise had existed in the beginning between an actuarially sound insurance scheme and a pay-as-you-go scheme, the former had clearly been abandoned by 1975. The latter was the basis of payouts. Today, the unfunded liability of existing social security is approximately $4 trillion, which raises the question of whether the system is bankrupt. The trust fund, or so-called reserve, has almost disappeared; and both the rate of taxation and the wage base have risen sharply in the last few years in order to pay for current obligations. Today the rate stands at 6.7 percent and is due to rise to 7.65 percent by 1990. The wage base has risen from $3000 at its inception to $32,400 in 1982.

Moreover, the funding problem will become more acute in future years because the aged will be a growing percentage of the total population. Today there are 30 retirees per 100 workers; but 40 years from now there will be 45 per 100, an increase of 50 percent. This change alone would require a 50 percent increase in the tax rate (on the assumption of an annual productivity increase of 2 percent).

How did this problem come about? The answer is a political-economic one. Retirees are voters, and politicians appealed to this group by offering larger benefits that accrued immediately, while the costs were deferred to a later time. Increased benefits appeared to be a free gift offered by the politician to a large and growing voter bloc. It is not surprising that historically the social security program has been a sacred cow of government, one of the most popular programs instituted in the New Deal era. But in the last decade, the popularity of the social security program has declined. Increasing voter opposition is evident everywhere. The windfall gains that accrued to politicians from expanding the social security program are now countered by the growing objections of those who are paying for it. Moreover, in the future the problem promises to become even more difficult. This is so for three reasons. First, the system is approaching maturity. Ninety-three percent of the population over 65 is receiving benefits. And the ratio of benefits to costs for new entrants into the system is much lower. A worker who entered the system in 1937 and paid the maximum tax for the next 30 years would have paid a total of $2,673.60 if he or she retired at the end of 1967. That would have been only a small fraction of the benefits received. But the worker who entered in 1968 and pays the maximum rate will have paid $27,512.25 after only 20 years. Assuming that the current scheduled increases in tax rates and wage base are not changed, the huge windfall gains that went to participants early in the program will come to an end, and many high-income workers will pay far more than the cost of their own benefits. Second, for a long period of time the program could increase its revenues simply by extending coverage. But now approximately 90 percent of the work force is covered; as a result, this option is no longer a significant source of new revenue. Third, Congress has in recent years **indexed** the benefit structure to make benefits increase as the price level increases. As long as earnings went up as fast as prices, the ratio remained constant. But in 1974, price increases exceeded wage increases; and the persistence of double-digit inflation and the era of **stagflation** in the 1970s resulted in a new dilemma.

Obviously, Congress now faces a very awkward situation. It is committed to paying social security benefits to a large and growing portion of the population. Moreover, the amounts that it will be forced to pay depend on economic events—the movement of wage and price—over which it has no direct control. It must therefore raise the social security taxes of a shrinking portion of the population to pay for benefits, while additional sources of revenue, other than straight tax increases, have dried up or have been deliberately sacrificed. It is easy to see why politicians squirm today when the social security issue comes up.

Earlier in this chapter the question was raised as to whether the social security program would go bankrupt. Martin Feldstein, a leading expert on the subject, has pointed out that the social security program is not bankrupt; "as long as the voters support the social security system, it will be able to pay the benefits is promises." Today, increasingly, there is a conflict of interest between the growing numbers of retirees on one hand and active workers on the other. Feldstein has estimated that of the 150 million Americans of voting age, 50 million will lose from social security and 100 million will gain; the latter, who are elderly, are more likely to vote in support of the program than are younger age groups.

In the past, the elderly have been much more concerned about social security than the younger groups. However, as the burden on the current workers grows, we can expect that to change. The system remains a viable one, but it does depend on the fundamental premise that workers accept an ever-growing obligation in taxes on their incomes. No doubt the social security program will be a continuing battleground of groups with conflicting interests, with politicians caught in the middle.

SUMMARY

Social security is a transfer system in which income is transferred from those who are working to those who are no longer working. The way in which social security is financed has little to do with the way in which benefits are received. Therefore, the "contributions" to social security should be viewed simply as another form of taxation. The political battle is between those who are receiving or who are about to receive benefits and those who must pay the taxes to provide those benefits.

DISCUSSION QUESTIONS

1. You are a member of Congress faced with restructuring the social security program. What would you do?
2. Would you favor a straight insurance program?

Glossary of Terms

Aggregate demand: The dollar value of planned expenditures for the economy on all final goods and services per year.

Aggregate supply: The total dollar value of all final goods and services supplied by firms to the market economy per year.

Antitrust legislation: The enactment of laws that restrict the formation of monopolies and regulate certain anticompetitive business practices.

Bond: An interest-bearing certificate issued by a government or a corporation. This type of security represents debt.

Capital: All manufactured resources, including buildings, equipment, machines, and improvements to land.

Capital gain: The positive difference between the purchase price and the sale price of an asset. If a share of stock is bought for $5 and then sold for $15, the capital gain is $10.

Commodity Credit Corporation: A government agency that "lends" farmers an amount of money equal to the support price of crops times the amount offered as collateral for the loan.

Common property: Property that is owned by everyone and therefore owned by no one. Examples of common property resources that have historically been owned in common are air and water.

Common stock: A security that indicates the real ownership in a corporation. A common stock is not a legal obligation for the firm and does not have a maturity. It has the last claim on dividends each year and on assets in the event of firm liquidation.

Competition: Rivalry among buyers and sellers of outputs, or among buyers and sellers of inputs.

Complements: Two goods are considered complements if a change in the price of one causes an opposite shift in the demand for the other. For example, if the price of tennis rackets goes up, the demand for tennis balls will fall; if the price of tennis rackets goes down, the demand for tennis balls will increase.

Consumer Price Index: A statistical measure of a weighted average of prices of a specified set of goods and services purchased by wage earners in urban areas.

Consumer sovereignty: The concept of the consumer as the one who, by his or her dollar votes, ultimately determines which goods and services will be produced in the economy. In principle, competition among producers causes them to adjust their production to the changing desires of consumers.

Deficit: The negative difference between inflows and outflows, or, more specifically, between income and expenditures; the term is often applied to government and called a government budget deficit.

Demand curve: A graphic representation of the demand schedule. A negatively sloped line showing the inverse relationship between the price and the quantity demanded.

Demand schedule: A set of pairs of numbers showing various possible prices and the quantities demanded at each price. This schedule shows the rate of planned purchases per time period at different prices of the good.

Discounting: A method by which account is taken of the lower value of a dollar in the future, compared to a dollar in hand today. Discounting is necessary even after adjustment for inflation because of the tradeoff between having more goods tomorrow if we consume less today.

Distribution of income: The way income is distributed among the population. For example, a perfectly equal distribution of income would result in the lowest 20 percent of income earners receiving 20 percent of national income and the top 20 percent also receiving 20 percent of national income. The middle 60 percent of income earners would receive 60 percent of national income.

Economic good: Any good or service that is scarce.

Economies of scale: Savings that result when output increases lead to decreases in long-run average costs.

Elastic demand: A characteristic of a demand curve in which a given percentage change in price will result in a larger percentage change in quantity demanded, in the opposite direction. Total revenues and price are inversely related in the elastic portion of the demand curve.

Equilibrium, or market-clearing, price: The price that clears the market where there is no excess quantity demanded or supplied. The price at which the demand curve intersects the supply curve.

Expansion: A business fluctuation in which overall business activity is rising at a more rapid rate than previously, or at a more rapid rate than the overall historical trend in a particular country.

Exploitation: The payment to a factor of production that is less than its value of marginal product.

Externalities: A situation in which a benefit or a cost associated with an economic activity spills over to third parties. Pollution is a negative spillover, or externality.

Fixed, or sunk, costs: Costs that do not vary with output. Fixed costs include items such as rent on a building and the price of machinery. These costs are fixed for a certain period of time; in the long run they are variable.

Free good: Any good or service that is available in quantities larger than are desired at a zero price.

Income elasticity of demand: The percentage change in the quantity demanded divided by the percentage change in money income; the responsiveness of the quantity demanded to changes in income.

Indexing: Inserting escalator, or cost-of-living, clauses into contracts, or tying contracts to the rate of inflation.

Inelastic demand: A characteristic of a demand curve in which a given change in price will result in a less-than-proportionate change in the quantity demanded, in the opposite direction. Total revenue and price are directly related in the inelastic region of the demand curve.

Inflation: A sustained rise in the weighted average of prices.

Inside information: Any kind of information that is available only to a few people, such as officers of a corporation.

Investment: The summation of fixed investment and inventory investment. Any addition to the future productive capacity of the economy.

Labor: Productive contributions of individuals who work, involving both thinking and doing.

Law of demand: A law that states that the quantity demanded and price are inversely related — more is bought at a lower price, less at a higher price (other things being equal).

Law of supply: A law that states that a direct relationship exists between price and the quantity supplied (other things being equal).

Liability: Anything that is owed.

Marginal costs: The change in total costs due to a change in one unit of production.

Marginal cost pricing: A system of pricing in which the price charged is equal to the opportunity cost to society of producing one more unit of the good or service in question. The opportunity cost is the marginal cost to society.

Market-clearing, or equilibrium, price: The price that clears the market when there is no excess quantity demanded or supplied. The price at which the demand curve intersects the supply curve.

Minimum wage: A legal wage rate below which employers cannot pay workers.

Models, or theories: Simplified representations of the real world used to make predictions or to better understand the real world.

Money supply: A generic term used to denote the amount of "money" in circulation. There are numerous specific definitions of the money supply. The narrowest is simply currency in the hands of the public plus demand deposits held only in commercial banks. This has been labeled the M1A money supply by the Federal Reserve System.

Monopolist: A single supplier.

Monopolistic competition: A market situation in which a large number of firms produce similar but not identical products, in which there is relatively easy entry into the industry.

Monopoly: A firm that has great control over the price of a good. In the extreme case, a monopoly is the only seller of a good or service.

Monopsonist: A single buyer.

Net worth: The difference between assets and liabilities.

Nominal, or absolute, price: The price observed today in terms of today's dollars. Also called nominal, or current, price.

Oligopoly: A market situation in which there are very few sellers, and in which each seller knows that the other sellers will react to its changes in prices and quantities.

Opportunity cost: The highest-valued alternative that must be sacrificed to attain something or satisfy a want.

Parity: A concept applied to the relative price of agricultural goods. The federal government has established parity by using a formula in which the price of agricultural goods was compared with the price of manufactured goods during the period 1910–1914. A parity price today would give farmers the same relative price for their products (compared to what they buy) that they received during the period 1910–1914.

Preferred stock: A security that indicates financing obtained from investors by a corporation. Preferred stock is not a legal obligation for the firm and does not have a maturity, but pays a fixed dividend each year. It has preferred position over common stock, both for dividends and for assets in the event of firm liquidation.

Price elasticity of demand: The responsiveness of the quantity demanded for a commodity to a change in its price per unit. Price elasticity of demand is defined as the percentage change in quantity demanded divided by the percentage change in price.

Price elasticity of supply: The responsiveness of the quantity supplied of a commodity to a change in its price per unit. Price elasticity of supply is defined as the percentage change in quantity supplied divided by the percentage change in price.

Price support: A minimum price set by the government. To be effective, price supports must be coupled with a mechanism to rid the market of "surplus" goods that arise whenever the supported price is greater than the market-clearing price.

Private costs: Costs incurred by individuals when they use scarce resources. For example, the private cost of running an automobile is equal to the gas, oil, insurance, maintenance, and depreciation costs. Also called explicit costs.

Profit: The income generated by selling something for a higher price than was paid for it. In production, the income generated is the difference between total revenues received from consumers who purchase the goods and the total cost of producing those goods.

Public information: Any kind of information that is widely available to the public.

Quota: A specified number of, or value of, imports allowed into a country per year.

Random walk: This refers to the situation in which future behavior cannot be predicted from past behavior. Stock prices follow a random walk.

Rationing: The term that refers to the government deciding, by means of some imposed method, who gets what. Typical government rationing schemes use ration coupons.

Recession: A period of time during which the rate of growth of business activity is consistently less than its long-term trend, or is negative.

Regressive tax: A tax in which, as more dollars are earned, the percentage of tax paid on them falls. In other words, the marginal tax rate is less than the average tax rate.

Relative price: The price of a commodity expressed in terms of the price of another commodity or the average price of all other commodities.

Resource: An input used in the production of goods and services desired.

Saving: The unspent portion of a consumer's income, or the difference between a consumer's income and his or her consumption expenditures.

Scarcity: A reference to the fact that at any point in time there exists only a finite amount of resources—human and non-human. Scarcity of resources means that nature does not freely provide as much of everything as people want.

Shortage: A situation in which an excess quantity is demanded or an insufficient quantity is supplied; the difference between the quantity demanded and the quantity supplied at a specific price below the market-clearing price.

Social costs: The full cost that society bears when a resource-using action occurs. For example, the social cost of driving a car is equal to all the private costs plus any additional cost that society bears, e.g., air pollution and traffic congestion.

Soil bank: The percentage of arable land that farmers must take out of production in order to receive price supports. In other words, a "bank" of unused soil.

Stagflation: A period of simultaneous high unemployment and rising prices. A combination of economic stagnation and inflation.

Stock: The quantity of something at a point in time. An inventory of goods is a stock. A bank account at a point in time is a stock. Stocks are defined independently of time although they are assessed at a point in time; savings is stock.

Subsidies: Negative taxes; payments to producers or consumers of a good or service. For example, farmers often get subsidies for producing wheat, corn, or peanuts.

Substitute: Two goods are considered substitutes when a change in the price of one causes a shift in demand for the other in the same direction as the price change. For example, if the price of butter goes up, the demand for margarine will rise; if the price of butter goes down, the demand for margarine will decrease.

Supply curve: The graphic representation of the supply schedule; a line showing the supply schedule, which slopes upward (has a positive slope).

Supply schedule: A set of prices, and the quantity supplied at each price; a schedule showing the rate of planned production of each relative price for a specified time period, usually one year.

Surplus: A term for an excess quantity supplied or an insufficient quantity demanded. The difference between the quantity supplied and the quantity demanded at a price above the market-clearing price.

Tariff: A tax on imported goods.

Tradeoff: A term relating to opportunity cost. In order to get a desired economic good, it is necessary to trade off some other desired economic good in a situation of scarcity. A tradeoff involves making a sacrifice in order to obtain something.

Union: An organization of workers that usually seeks to secure economic improvements for its members.

Value of marginal product: The change in total revenues that results from a unit change in a variable input; also equal to marginal physical product times marginal revenue, or MPP × MR.

Variable costs: Costs that vary with the rate of production. They include wages paid to workers, the cost of materials, and so on.

Index

83 84 85 86 9 8 7 6 5 4 3 2 1